Homemade for HAMSTERS

Homemade for HAMSTERS

Over 20 Fun Projects Anyone Can Make, Including Tunnels, Towers, Dens, Swings, Ladders and More

Carin Oliver

FIREFLY BOOKS

A FIREFLY BOOK

Published by Firefly Books Ltd. 2016

First printing

Publisher Cataloging-in-Publication Data (U.S.)

Names: Oliver, Carin, author.
Title: Homemade for hamsters : over 20 fun projects anyone can make, including tunnels, towers, dens, swings, ladders and more / Carin Oliver.
Description: Richmond Hill, Ontario, Canada : Firefly Books, 2016. | Includes index. | Summary: "Packed with illustrations and easy-to-follow instructions, this book includes over 20 fun projects for creating toys and exercise equipment for your hamster, using materials commonly found around the home" — Provided by publisher.
Identifiers: ISBN 978-1-77085-781-0 (paperback)
Subjects: LCSH: Hamsters — Juvenile literature. | Hamsters as pets — Juvenile literature. | Hamsters — Behavior — Juvenile literature.
Classification: LCC SF459.H3O458 |DDC 636.9356 – dc23

Library and Archive Canada Cataloguing in Publication

Oliver, Carin, author
Homemade for hamsters : over 20 fun projects anyone can make, including tunnels, towers, dens, swings, ladders and more / Carin Oliver.
Includes index.
ISBN 978-1-77085-781-0 (paperback)
1. Pet supplies--Juvenile literature. 2. Handicrafts--Juvenile literature. 3. Hamsters as pets--Juvenile literature. I. Title.
SF413.5.O55 2016 j745.5 C2016-900070-2

Published in the United States by
Firefly Books (U.S.) Inc.
P.O. Box 1338, Ellicott Station
Buffalo, New York 14205

Published in Canada by
Firefly Books Ltd.
50 Staples Avenue, Unit 1
Richmond Hill, Ontario L4B 1H1

Conceived, edited and designed by
Marshall Editions
The Old Brewery
6 Blundell Street, London N7 9BH

Senior Editor: Julia Shone
Senior Art Editor: Emma Clayton
Designer: Karin Skånberg
Photographer: Simon Pask
Illustrator: Charlotte Farmer
Proofreader: Claudia Martin
Indexer: Helen Snaith
Art Director: Caroline Guest
Creative Director: Moira Clinch
Publisher: Paul Carslake

Color separation by
Cypress Colours (HK) Ltd, Hong Kong
Printed by Toppan Leefung Printing Ltd, China

CONTENTS

1 GETTING STARTED

Getting prepared for making exercise equipment and toys for your hamster is easy — all you'll need are a few tools and materials, many of which you probably already have on hand. Knowing how to set up and maintain a safe and enriching environment will help you to give your pet a happy and long life. In this chapter, you'll find details of the building materials and tools that you'll need, along with some basic techniques and recipes to get you started.

PLANNING YOUR PROJECTS AND EXERCISE TIME

Making and maintaining exercise equipment that will suit your particular hamster requires just a little planning and some regular attention to keep things in good shape.

Sizing

Be sure to size your toys so that your hamster can use them comfortably, without fear of getting stuck. Entrance holes should be sized so that your hamster can fit through with room to spare. When building a tunnel system, try out a test piece with your hamster first to be sure that the tube is wide enough so that there is no chance of getting stuck, even with cheek pouches stuffed with food.

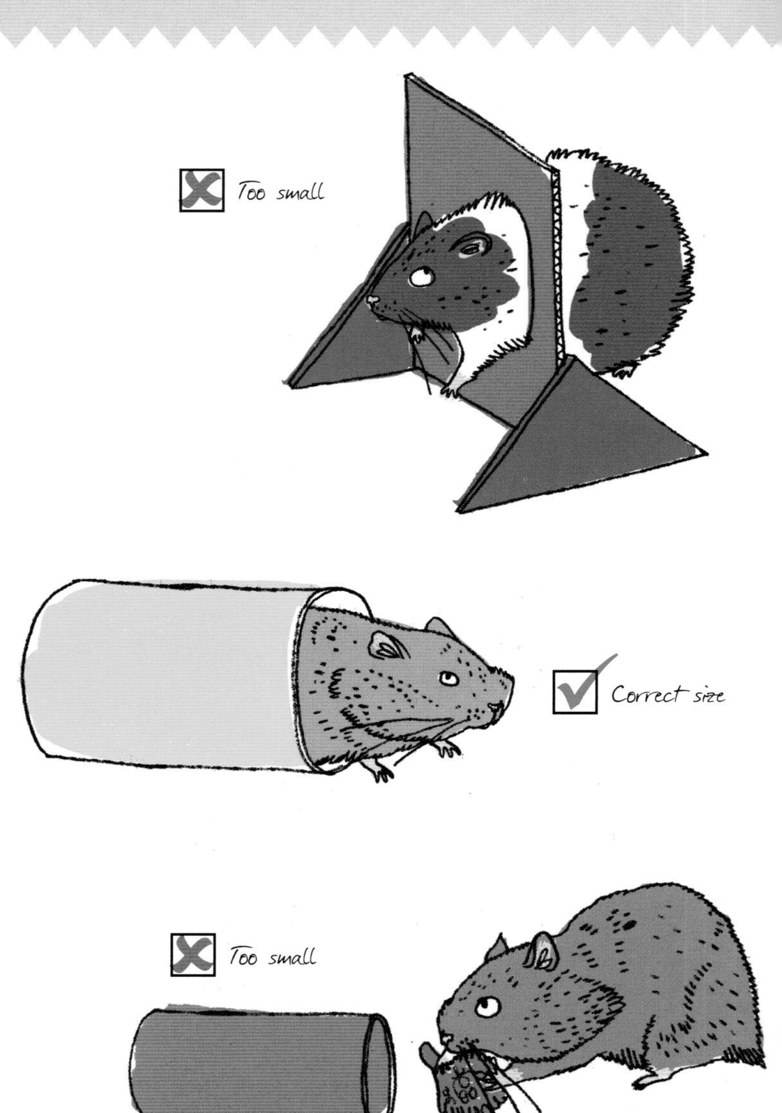

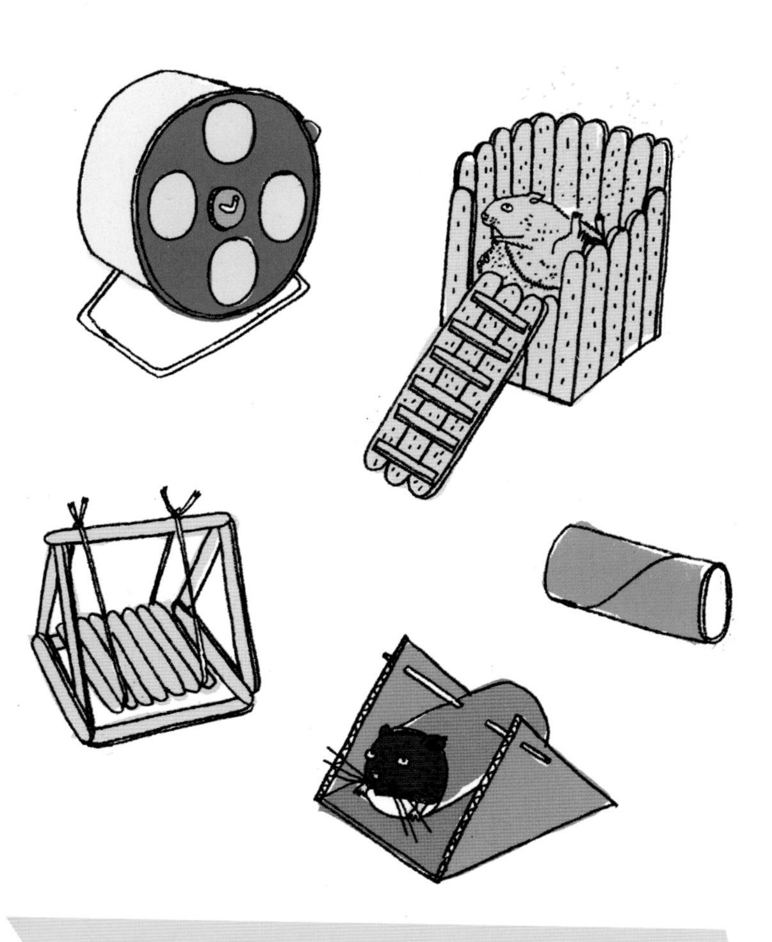

Supervise Exercise

Hamsters benefit from regular exercise time out of their cages. Using the projects in this book, you can set up a terrific playground filled with a variety of activities to give your hamster a great workout. Always supervise your hamster's exercise sessions — it keeps them safe and is a great way to spend time with your pet.

Watching them play also allows you to learn which kinds of toys your pet enjoys the most. Before letting your hamster out, make sure that you have hamster-proofed the room and eliminated any avenues for escape, such as open windows or doors, or closets filled with hiding places.

Safety Check and Maintenance

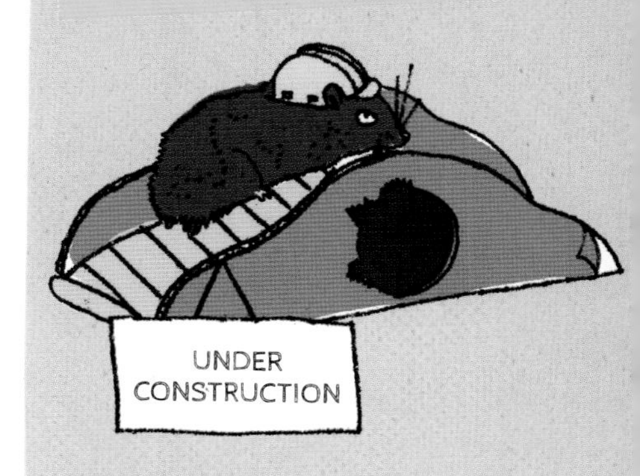

As you collect materials and build your projects, eliminate any sharp or ragged edges that could hurt your hamster or invite nibbling. Toys and hideouts should be checked on a regular basis to make sure they are in good condition — repair or replace any chewed or worn toys, and check hideouts regularly for any stored food that may be rotting.

BASIC TECHNIQUES AND RECIPES

Here, you'll find some helpful working tips, as well as recipes for hamster-safe glue and dye. Review these before getting started, and your finished projects will look great and be safe.

Making Vegetable Dye

You can use store-bought natural food coloring to paint hamster toys, but you can also make your own using fruits and vegetables:

1 Shred or chop the fruit or vegetables into small pieces.

2 Put the water in the blender and add the vegetables. For a stronger color, use less water. Blend until the vegetables are very finely chopped and almost a smooth consistency.

3 Pour the mixture through a strainer into a bowl to remove the pulp. The resulting dye can be used on wood or paper.

YOU WILL NEED

* Hamster-safe fruit or vegetables in the color you want (see Choosing Your Hamster Treats, page 13)
* Approximately 1 cup (250 ml) water
* Grater or kitchen knife
* Blender
* Mesh strainer

Folding

Making a clean fold in thick materials such as cardboard can be tricky. Doing an extra step or two can make the end result better:

1 Working on the side of the cardboard that will be the outside of the folded shape, use a ruler to measure and draw a line where you'd like the fold to be.

2 Place the ruler along the line. Using gentle pressure, lightly score a line across the material. Be careful not to cut all the way through.

3 Flip the cardboard over and then measure and draw a line in the same place. Holding the ruler next to the line, fold the cardboard up.

Gluing

The most important thing to remember when gluing is to wait for the glue to set before moving on to the next stage of the construction.

1 Protect the work surface with a scrap piece of paper or cardboard.

2 When using bottled glue, open the top only halfway rather than all the way, to prevent accidentally squeezing excess glue onto your project.

3 Use enough glue to hold the parts together. Press the parts together while the glue dries by taping parts together temporarily or weighting with a heavy book or using a bulldog clip to clamp the join while it dries. Leave the construction until fully dry.

Papier Mâché Paste and Nontoxic Glue

This recipe makes a nice smooth paste that can be used to glue paper or to make papier mâché. Store it in the refrigerator if you won't be using it all right away.

1 Place the flour in a bowl and add the salt along with 1 cup (250 ml) of the water. Mix well.

2 In a saucepan, boil the remaining 2 cups (500 ml) of water. Once boiling, slowly add the flour-and-water mixture. Boil and stir for 2–3 minutes.

3 Allow to cool slightly. If it is too thick, slowly add a little water to thin it to the desired consistency.

YOU WILL NEED

* 1 cup (250 ml) flour
* ¼ tsp. (1 ml) salt
* 3 cups (750 ml) water

Cutting with a Utility Knife

Utility knives are a good way to cut materials that are too thick for scissors, but should only be used by adults as they are very sharp.

1 Protect the surface of your work table with a cutting mat or scrap piece of cardboard.

2 If the knife has a locking blade, make sure that it is locked securely in place before use. When cutting, keep your other hand out of the path of the blade.

3 Cut using gentle pressure and make several passes, if necessary. Always retract the blade when you have finished cutting.

NOTE:

If you are cutting against a ruler for a straight edge, always use a steel ruler rather than plastic.

Sanitizing Twigs Collected from Outdoors

You can use twigs and branches to make hamster toys but first they need to be sterilized to kill any bacteria or parasites.

1 Collect twigs only from hamster-safe trees, such as deciduous trees like willow, beech, maple, birch, hazelnut, pear and apple. Avoid collecting from fruit trees that have been sprayed or from trees near a road, where there are exhaust fumes.

2 Remove all loose bark and debris.

3 Bake in the oven at 250°F (120°C) for 2–3 hours.

MAKING HAMMIE FEEL AT HOME

Building and arranging a cage for your hamster is the first step in making your little furry friend comfortable in his/her new surroundings. Here are some basic guidelines for creating a safe and fun environment for your hammie to live in.

NEST WITH BEDDING
A hamster needs a secure nest filled with safe bedding (such as the Hideaway Cave, see pages 80-81) to sleep during the day.

A CLIMBING WALL
Hamsters love to climb, so why not indulge your pet's vertical acrobatics? The wooden Climbing Wall (see pages 40-41) can be carefully attached to the cage's bars or a platform.

FOOD
Use specialist hamster food — either compound pellets or a mixture of different cereals and seeds. The food should be placed in a flat dish or directly onto the floor.

WATER BOTTLE
The most commonly used water bottles have a sipper tube. The water should be changed daily and the bottle kept clean.

SUBSTRATE
The cage bottom should be lined with a substrate material (such as wood shavings) to absorb urine. Hamsters love digging, so keep it to 1 in. (2.5 cm) deep. Provide extra stimulation by scattering food to encourage foraging.

TUBES
Tubes replicate the natural environment of burrows in the wild and offer a safe space for your pet to retreat to.

GNAWING TOYS
Hamsters' teeth grow continuously, so gnawing is essential to keep them trim. The Walnut Shell Toy (see pages 70-71) is not only perfect for gnawing but also for encouraging your hamster's natural foraging behavior.

PLATFORM
Platforms can be added to provide more floor space within the cage. Always make sure that they are properly secured to the cage frame.

TREAT BALL
(See pages 74-75) This toy helps keep your hamster stimulated by making him/her work for treats. The cardboard is also great for gnawing.

BENDY BRIDGE
(See pages 52-53) This enables your hammie to reach the different levels of the cage.

ADDITIONAL HOUSE
(Optional) Hamsters love relaxing in small, enclosed and dark places, since this is where they feel the safest. The Hammie Hill (see pages 82-85) provides an enticing retreat, as well as an opportunity for them to exercise and explore.

CAGE
The minimum recommended size for hamster cages is 155 sq. in. (1,000 cm²) of floor space and a height of 7.5 in. (19 cm) for Syrian hamsters, and 115 sq. in. (750 cm²) of usable floor space with a height of 6.5 in. (17 cm) for Dwarfs. Buy the largest cage that you can in order to provide your hamster with plenty of space.

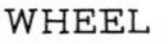

WHEEL
This is essential for hammies (see The Wheel, pages 28-31). Always make sure that the wheel is large enough to comfortably accommodate your pet.

CHOOSING YOUR HAMSTER TREATS

On pages 68–77, you'll find a selection of chewing toy projects. These often incorporate treats hidden within the toy, which encourage hammie to chew. Knowing which foods are safe to give to your hamster is crucial. Please note: this is not an exhaustive list!

SAFE TREATS

* Apples (but not seeds)
* Bananas
* Blackberries
* Blueberries
* Broccoli
* Carrots
* Coconut
* Dried meal worms
* Mango
* Nuts — almonds (must be shelled); Brazil nuts; cashews; monkey nuts; pecans; walnuts
* Raisins
* Spinach
* Strawberries
* Sunflower seeds — only as a special treat since they are high in fat
* Timothy hay — extra fiber
* Watermelon

UNSAFE TREATS

* Tomato leaves
* Beans and potatoes — often lead to diarrhea
* Onions, garlic and peppers
* All citrus fruits — too acidic for hamsters
* All junk food
* Sugary foods (glucose, honey etc.)
* Chocolate/peanut butter/all candy

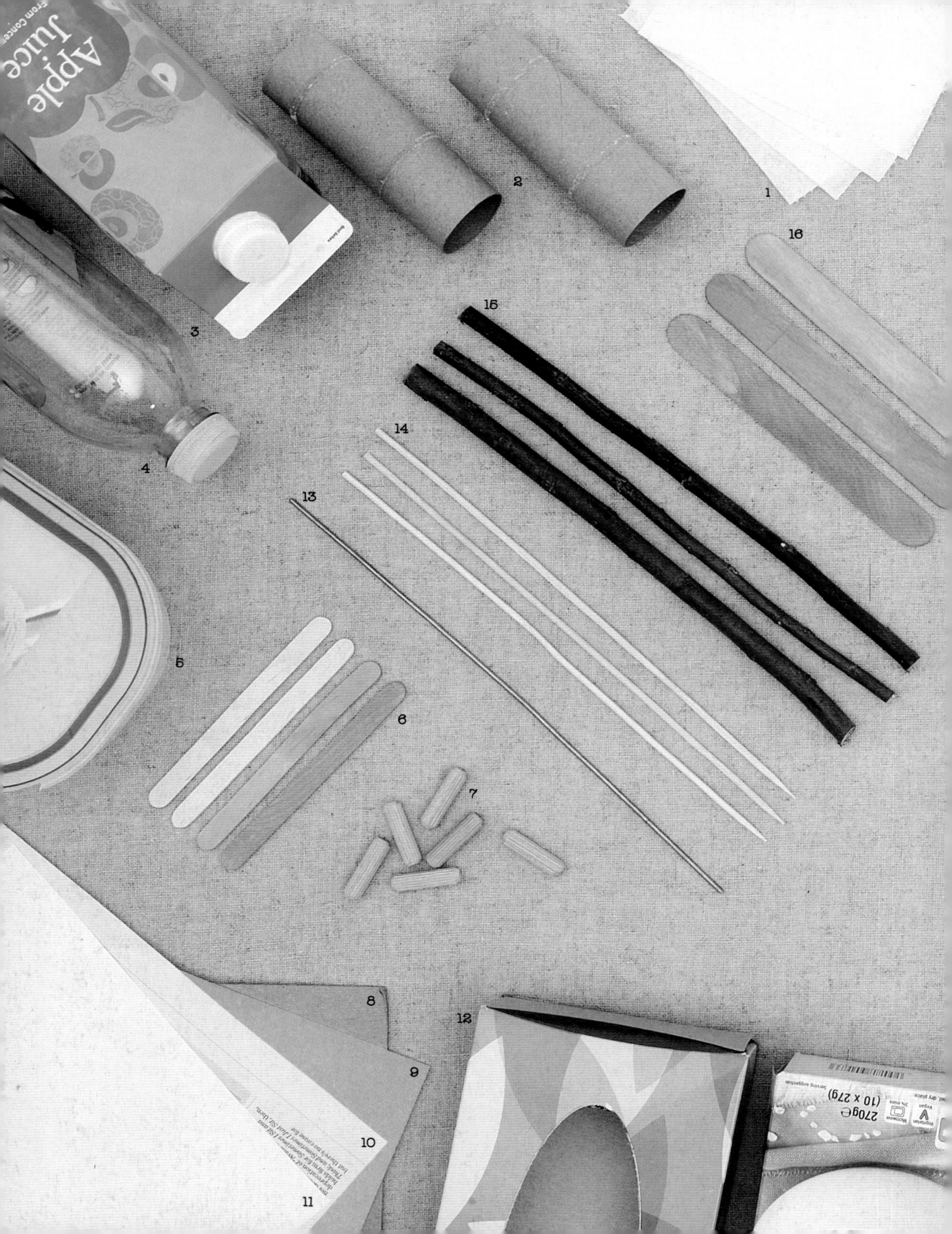

1
2
Apple Juice
3
4
5
6
7
8
9
10
11
12
270g℮ (10 x 27g)
13
14
15
16

BUILDING MATERIALS

All of the building materials are easy to come by. In fact, you'll probably find that you already have most of these items around the house but, if you don't, then they can be easily sourced at a hardware or craft-supply store.

TOILET/TISSUE PAPER (1)
Make sure that it is unscented and not dyed.

TOILET PAPER TUBES (2)
Plain cardboard tubes are easy to come by and make great toys by themselves.

JUICE OR MILK CARTONS (3)
These containers have a waxy coating that makes them good for hamster toys containing sand, but you must ensure that you don't let your hamster eat them.

CLEAR PLASTIC BOTTLES (4)
These are good for building see-through tunnels, but take care not to leave these in your hamster's cage where they can be chewed.

CLEAR PLASTIC FOOD CONTAINERS OR CLEAR PLASTIC FOOD PACKAGING (5)
Useful as parts of a see-through adventure maze, but, again, do not leave these in your hamster's cage unsupervised.

POPSICLE STICKS (6)
If you're collecting these as you consume Popsicles, make sure they're clean before you use them! Or, you can purchase these new at a craft store. Add color with vegetable-based dye (see page 10).

WOODEN DOWELS (7)
These come in many different sizes and can be purchased at craft stores.

CORRUGATED CARDBOARD (8)
You can re-use cardboard from packing boxes. Look for boxes with less ink printed on them, as these will be safer for your hamster to play with.

CONSTRUCTION PAPER (9)
Look for this colored paper with soy-based inks. However, if your hamster really likes to eat paper, then it would be better to use white paper and color with vegetable-based dyes made using the recipe provided in the Basic Techniques (see page 10).

NEWSPAPER (10)
Stick to black-and-white printed newspaper, and avoid color and glossy pages.

WHITE COPY PAPER (11)
If you have a home printer, you're sure to have some of this but, if not, it's easy to source from any local store.

SMALL CARDBOARD BOXES (12)
Empty tissue boxes or cardboard food containers are ideal. Again, try to use boxes with less ink printed on them.

STURDY WIRE (13)
You can either use wire from a coat hanger or purchase thinner wire at a hardware store.

BAMBOO SKEWERS (14)
These are easy to find in your local grocery store, and they often come in large and small sizes.

STICKS SOURCED FROM OUTSIDE (15)
Make sure that you stick to deciduous trees such as willow, beech, maple, pear and apple. Don't use twigs from fruit trees sprayed with insecticide or gather twigs near a road, as they could be contaminated by exhaust fumes.

JUMBO CRAFT STICKS (16)
Especially useful if you have a larger-sized hamster and want to build bigger structures for him/her.

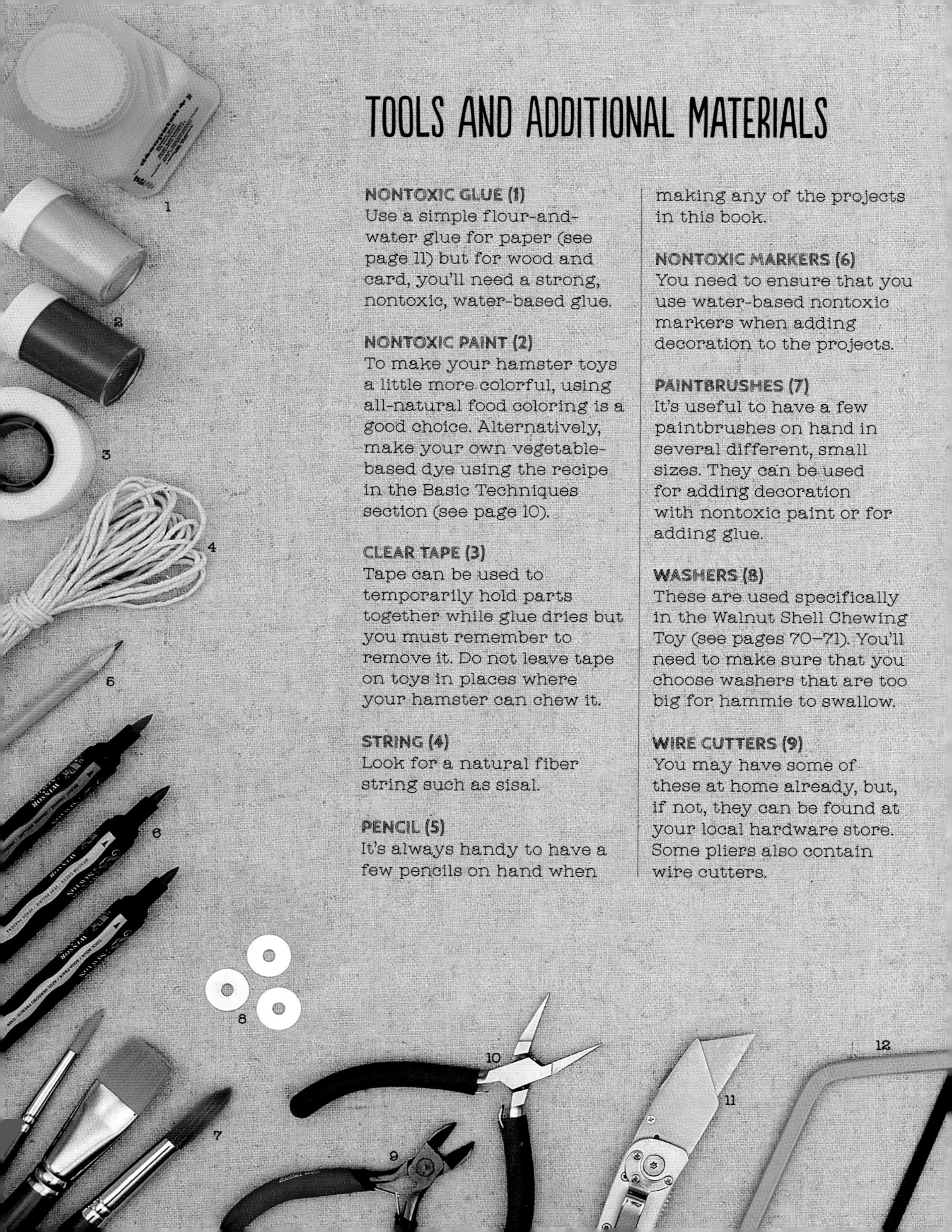

TOOLS AND ADDITIONAL MATERIALS

NONTOXIC GLUE (1)
Use a simple flour-and-water glue for paper (see page 11) but for wood and card, you'll need a strong, nontoxic, water-based glue.

NONTOXIC PAINT (2)
To make your hamster toys a little more colorful, using all-natural food coloring is a good choice. Alternatively, make your own vegetable-based dye using the recipe in the Basic Techniques section (see page 10).

CLEAR TAPE (3)
Tape can be used to temporarily hold parts together while glue dries but you must remember to remove it. Do not leave tape on toys in places where your hamster can chew it.

STRING (4)
Look for a natural fiber string such as sisal.

PENCIL (5)
It's always handy to have a few pencils on hand when making any of the projects in this book.

NONTOXIC MARKERS (6)
You need to ensure that you use water-based nontoxic markers when adding decoration to the projects.

PAINTBRUSHES (7)
It's useful to have a few paintbrushes on hand in several different, small sizes. They can be used for adding decoration with nontoxic paint or for adding glue.

WASHERS (8)
These are used specifically in the Walnut Shell Chewing Toy (see pages 70–71). You'll need to make sure that you choose washers that are too big for hammie to swallow.

WIRE CUTTERS (9)
You may have some of these at home already, but, if not, they can be found at your local hardware store. Some pliers also contain wire cutters.

PLIERS (10)
For bending and twisting wire, these are particularly useful if you are working with really thick wire.

UTILITY KNIFE (11)
Useful for cutting corrugated cardboard, this tool should only ever be used by an adult with extreme care.

SMALL CRAFT SAW (12)
This is the best tool for cutting sticks and dowels. It should be handled with care and used only on an appropriate, sturdy and supported surface.

HAMMER (13)
A small tack hammer is sufficient for the projects in this book.

RULER (14)
A ruler is useful for measuring pieces large enough to suit your hamster. It can also be useful as a straight edge for cutting with a utility knife, but you'll need to ensure that you use a steel ruler rather than a plastic one for this purpose.

NAILS (15)
Medium and larger sizes are useful for punching holes in things, such as in the Walnut Shell Chewing Toy (see pages 70–71).

SANDPAPER (16)
This is for ensuring that you smooth off any rough edges when building pieces from plastic. Use a medium grit, such as 120.

DECORATIVE PAPER (17)
Use sparingly as your hamster can chew on it, and avoid using paper with puffy paint, glitter or any other decorations glued to it.

SCISSORS (18)
A good, sturdy pair works best for cutting thick materials.

There are a few key tools and materials that you'll need to complete the projects described in this book. Once you've collected these items, you'll have a basic toolkit that will allow you to build away to your heart's content.

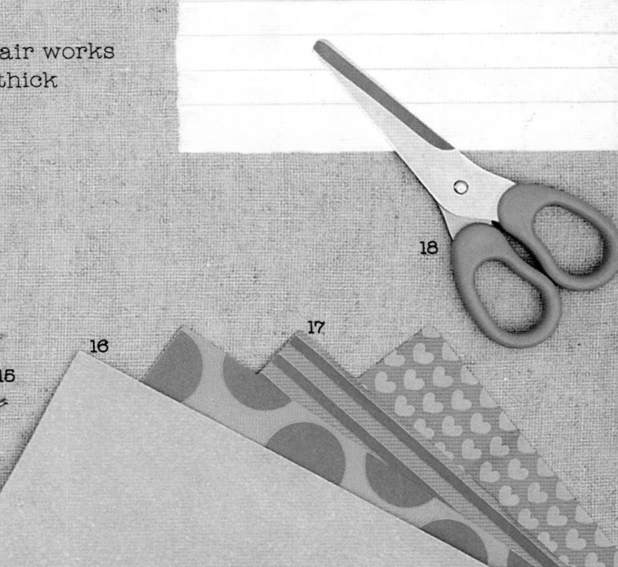

14

13

2 THE PROJECTS

In this chapter, you'll find instructions and ideas for 21 delightful projects that you can build for your hamster, divided into five sections according to activity: running, climbing, digging, chewing and resting.

RUNNING PROJECTS

It's an inherent part of a hamster's nature to be on the move, and in the wild they travel long distances on a daily basis to patrol their territory and search for food. In this section, you will find lots of project ideas to help provide your pet with the essential, regular exercise that he/she needs.

THE TUNNEL

You can easily keep an eye on your hammie while he/she runs through this tunnel as it is made with clear plastic drink bottles and containers.

TOOLS & MATERIALS

* Large, clear plastic drink bottles
* Scissors
* Clear tape

OPTIONAL:

* Square clear plastic food containers for connecting multiple tunnels
* Nontoxic markers

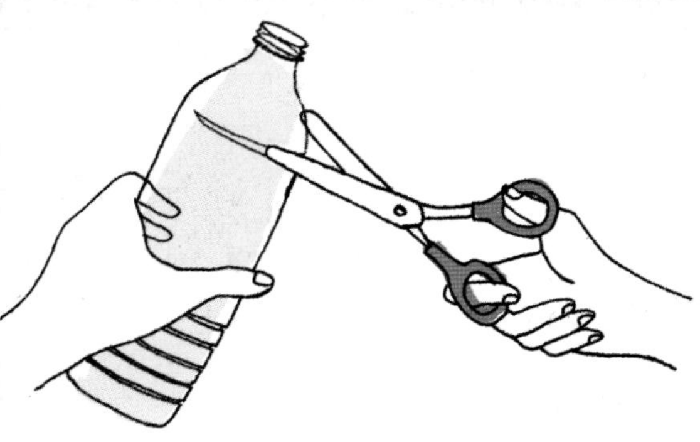

1 Wash all bottles and containers thoroughly, removing any labels. Using scissors, carefully cut off the tops of all the bottles at the point where they begin to curve. Make sure that you don't leave any ragged edges. Supervise children during steps 1 and 2.

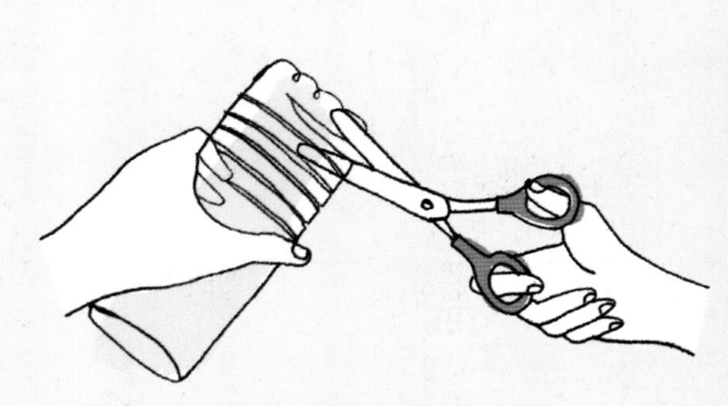

2 Cut the bottoms off the bottles at the widest point, so that you are left with the biggest possible opening.

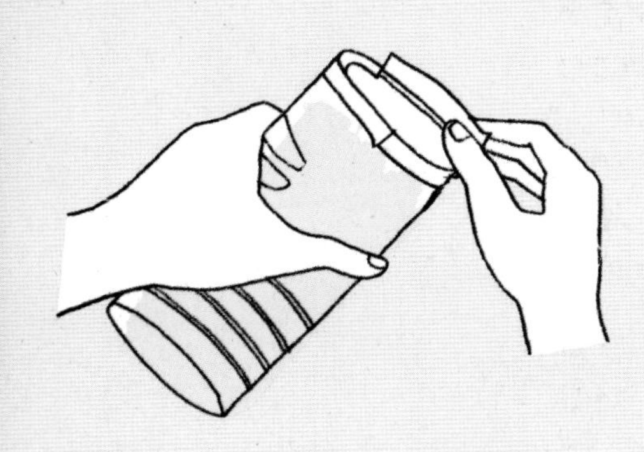

3 For your hamster's protection, cover every cut edge securely with clear tape.

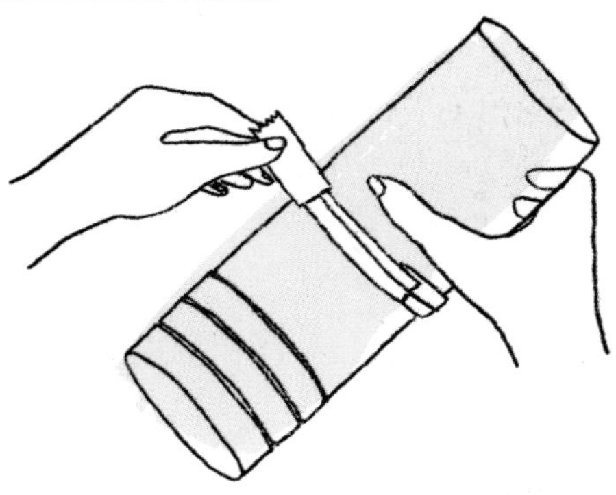

4 Slot the smaller top end of one bottle into the bigger bottom end of another. Place clear tape all the way around the seam. Repeat this process, attaching several bottles together to make a tunnel.

5 You can use an empty square container to change the direction of your tunnel. Trace the size of the tunnel opening on one side of the square container and cut out this shape. Insert the tunnel and tape in place. Repeat this on another side of the square container and build a tunnel in another direction.

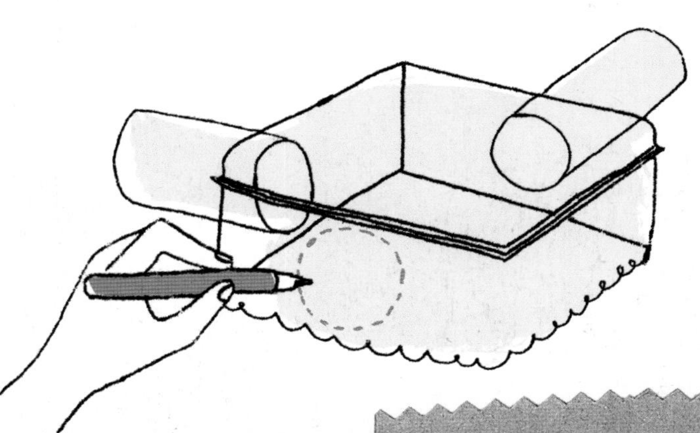

AMAZING MAZE

In the wild, hamsters live in a network of underground tunnels and rooms. You can give your pet hamster a similar kind of exercise and challenge by making a cardboard maze. This is an ideal activity for an energetic and curious creature and, of course, there's a reward at the end!

TOOLS & MATERIALS

* Cardboard
* Scissors or utility knife
* Cutting mat
* Ruler
* Strong, nontoxic glue
* Pencil
* Non-sugary cereal or other treat

OPTIONAL:

* Construction paper, stickers or nontoxic markers

Mondrian-style hamster maze

1 Using scissors or a utility knife, cut a piece of cardboard to the size you want your maze floor to be.

2 Cut four strips of cardboard for the outside walls. Two strips should match the length of the maze floor and two strips should match the width of the maze floor.

3 Using a pencil and ruler, draw a design for the maze on the floor. Be sure to include some dead ends and split paths to make it challenging for the hamster.

4 Glue the four strips of cardboard to the outside edges of the maze floor to form the outside walls.

KEEP IT INTERESTING

Put a turning before each dead end, so that your hamster can't see it.

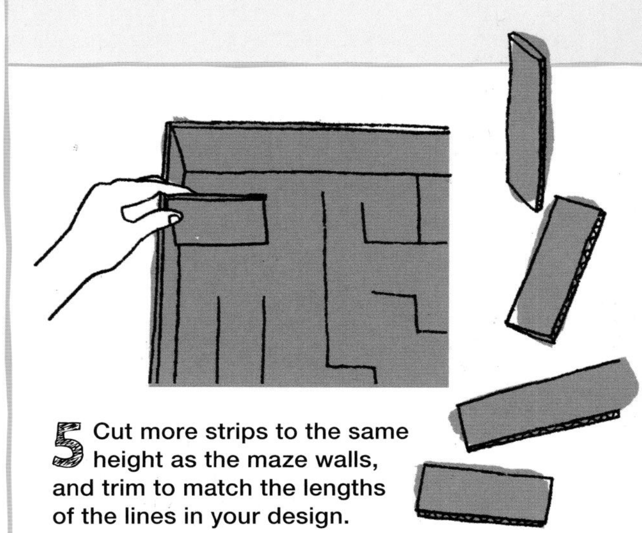

5 Cut more strips to the same height as the maze walls, and trim to match the lengths of the lines in your design.

6 Glue these strips in place to make the maze corridor walls.

7 Cut one final strip to fit snugly between the walls near the start of the maze. You will slide this in and out of place to create a starting pen, so don't glue it in!

8 Place treats or cereal at the end of the maze. Then lift up the starting gate, and watch the hamster go! Always supervise your hamster while in the maze.

Optional

Before you assemble them, decorate the maze walls with stickers, construction paper or nontoxic markers — see the photos shown here for inspiration. Just make sure that your hamster doesn't eat the decorations!

ADD A SEE-THROUGH LID

Does your hamster "cheat" by climbing over the maze walls? If so, set a sheet of glass or clear plastic over the top of the maze. Ensure that there are gaps or air holes.

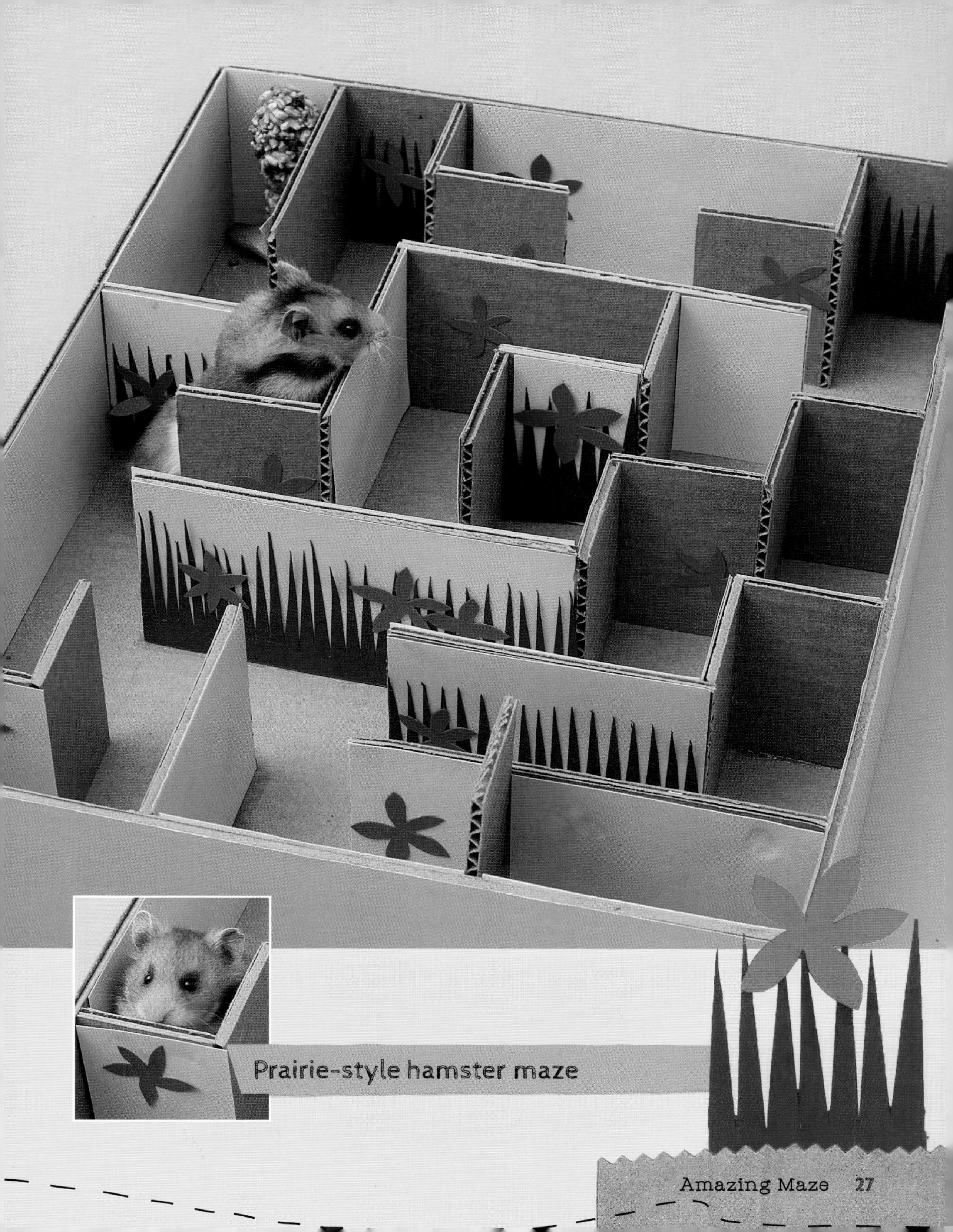

Prairie-style hamster maze

THE WHEEL

Hamsters were born to run and this project is a great way for your hamster to burn off some energy. A hamster in the wild can run for several miles a day, so imagine how many spins of the wheel that would be!

TOOLS & MATERIALS

* Round plastic container with a lid, such as a margarine tub (large enough for hammie to run in without arching his/her back)
* Sturdy wire, approx. 2 ft. (60 cm) long — you can use a coat hanger, cut and straightened
* Utility knife
* Sandpaper
* Pliers
* Wire cutters
* Pencil
* Corrugated cardboard
* Scissors

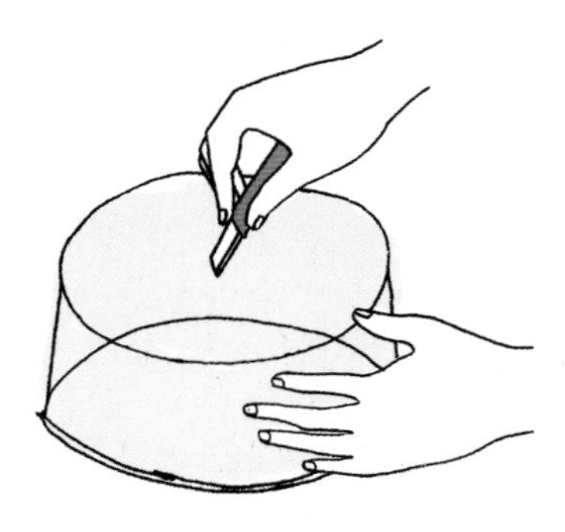

1 Wash the plastic container thoroughly. Poke a small hole in the center of the container bottom with a utility knife or the end of the wire.

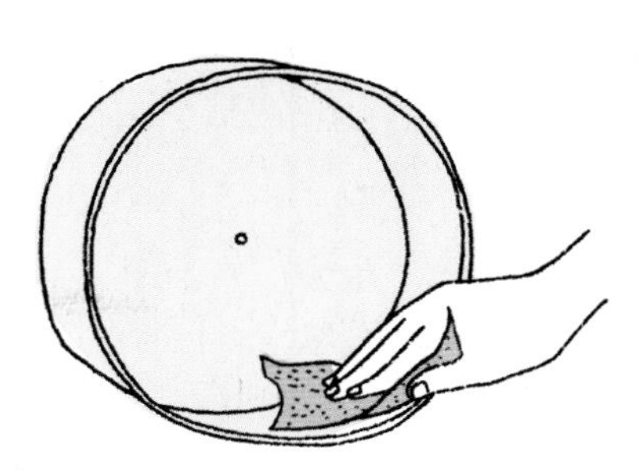

2 If the inside of the container is very smooth, sand along the sides so that your hamster won't slip once inside the moving wheel.

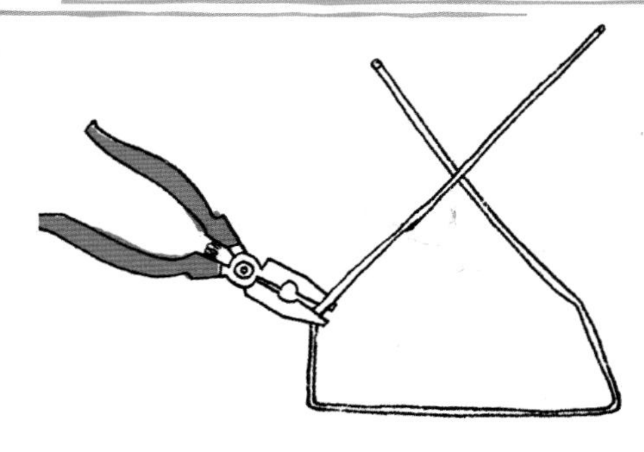

3 Using pliers, bend the wire to form three sides of a rectangle, approximately the width of the container. Bend the remaining ends of wire into the shape of an "X" with the cross at the height of the center of your wheel. This creates your base.

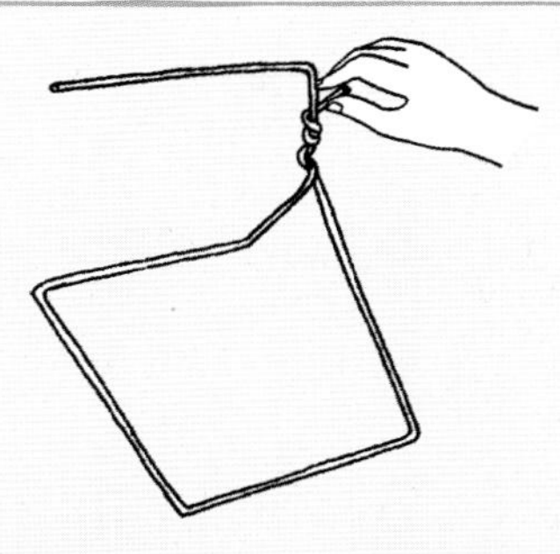

4 At the point of the cross, twist the remaining end of one wire around the other and trim off with wire cutters. Bend the other end of wire over at a right angle. This will become the axle of the wheel.

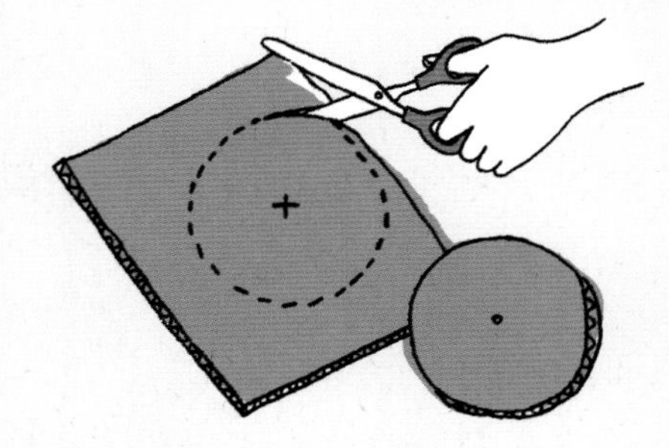

5 Draw two circles of approximately 1½ in. (3.8 cm) in diameter onto the corrugated cardboard and cut out with scissors. Use the wire to poke a hole in the center of each circle.

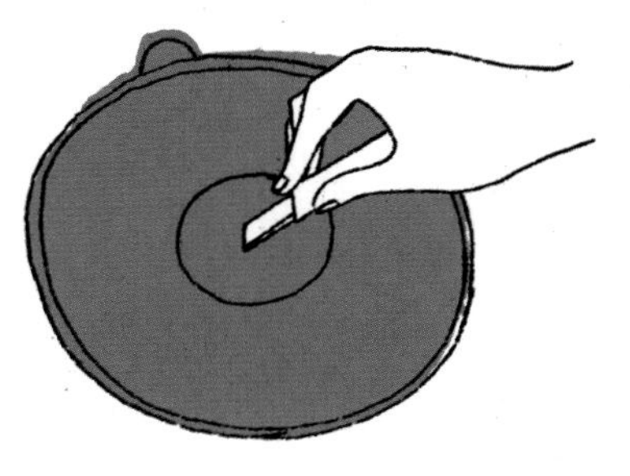

6 Using a utility knife, poke a hole in the center of the container lid, large enough to fit the wire through.

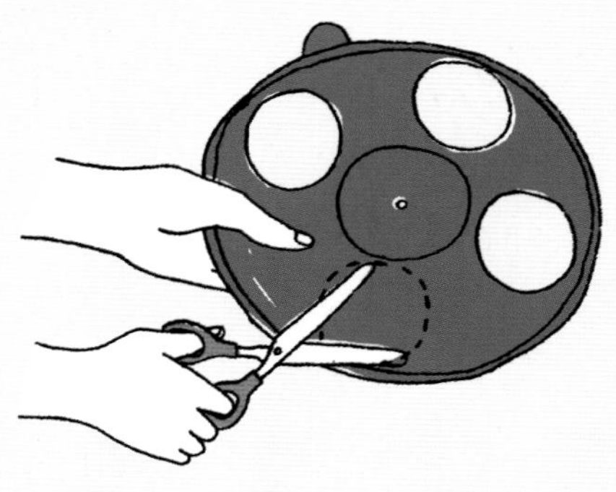

7 Cut out four holes near the outer edge of the lid, large enough for your hamster to easily fit through. Supervise children during step 7.

WHEEL SIZES

Small hamsters, such as dwarf varieties, will need a wheel of approximately 6½ in. (16.5 cm) in diameter, while larger breeds, such as a Syrian, will need a wheel of 8 in. (20 cm) or more.

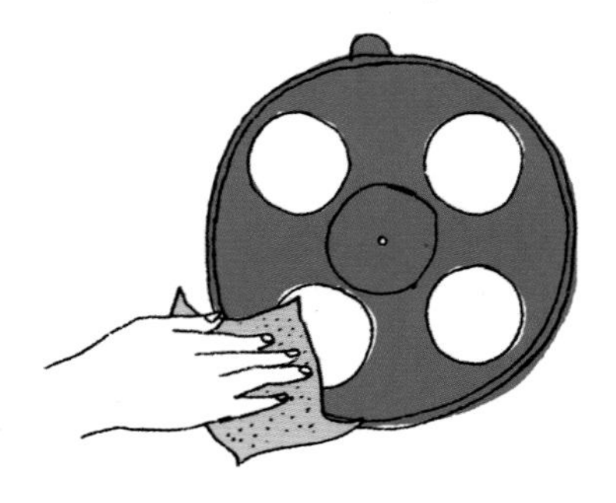

8 Using sandpaper, sand the edges of each hole to remove any sharp spots. Put the lid onto the container.

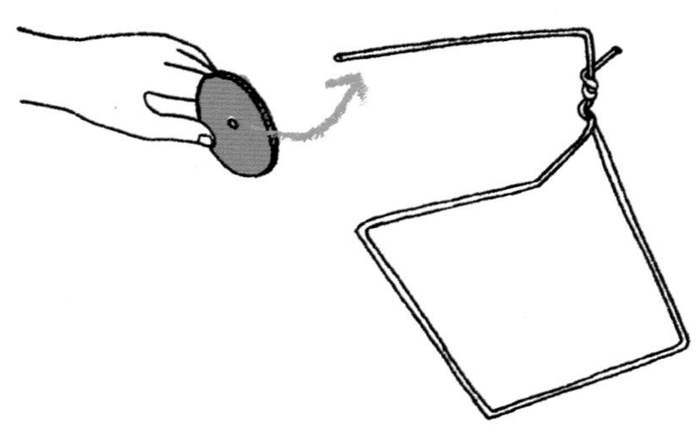

9 Stick one of the cardboard circles onto the wire axle before adding the container and the lid. Spin to make sure the wheel moves freely. If not, remove from the axle and make the holes in the container and the lid a little bigger.

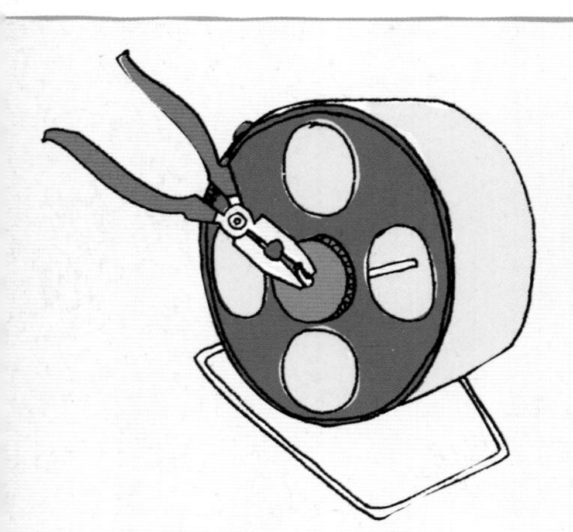

10 Place the other cardboard circle on the wire axle and then bend the end of the axle down to keep everything in place.

THE OBSTACLE COURSE

Hamsters are smart creatures and so they can easily learn to use an obstacle course. This course includes four obstacles: a Window Jump, an A-Frame Ladder, a Bar Jump and a Seesaw. You can add other pieces to your course if you want, such as a simple tunnel made from a cardboard tube.

TOOLS & MATERIALS

* Popsicle sticks
* Strong, nontoxic glue
* Corrugated cardboard
* Scissors
* Ruler
* Jumbo craft sticks
* Wooden dowel
* Small craft saw
* Pencil

OPTIONAL:

* Nontoxic markers or paint

Window Jump

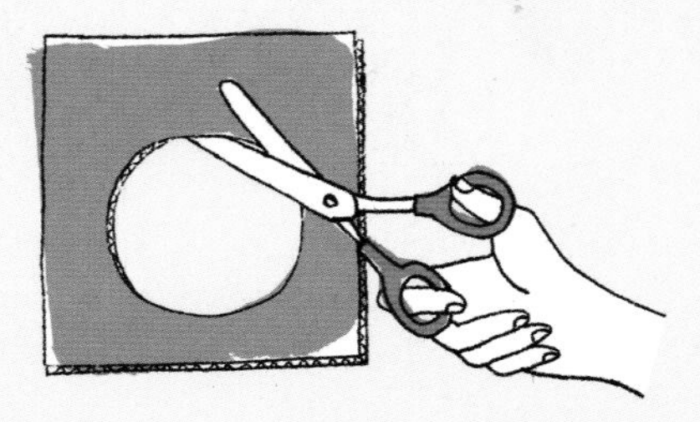

1 Cut out a rectangle of corrugated cardboard of approximately 3½ x 3 in. (9 x 7.5 cm). At an inch or so from the bottom, cut out a circular hole that is large enough for your hamster to crawl through.

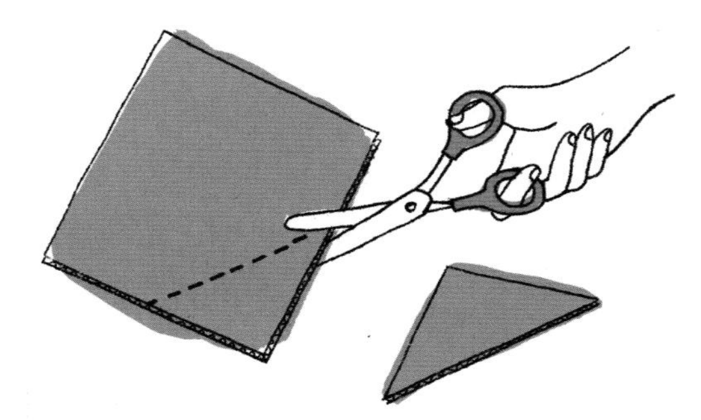

2 Cut out two small triangles from the corrugated cardboard — the longest side should be at least 3 in. (7.5 cm) long. These triangles will act as the base of the jump.

3 Glue one triangle, longest side down, on either side of the window jump.

A-Frame Ladder

1 Glue the ends of two Popsicle sticks together at an angle to create a bridge. Make the angle shallow enough for your hamster to run up one side and down the other side.

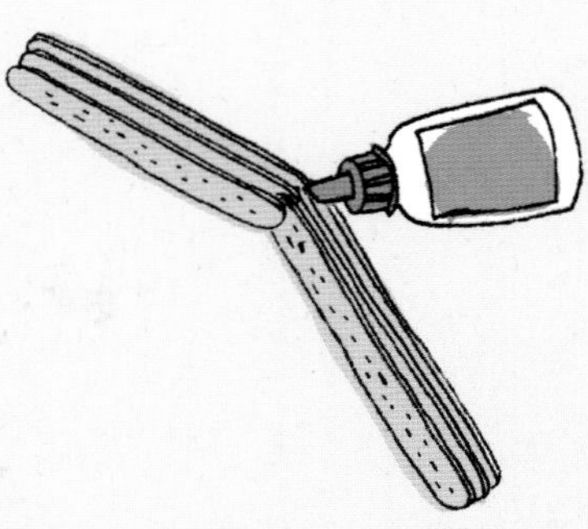

2 Glue four alternating layers of sticks so that the bridge is wide enough to stand up on its own.

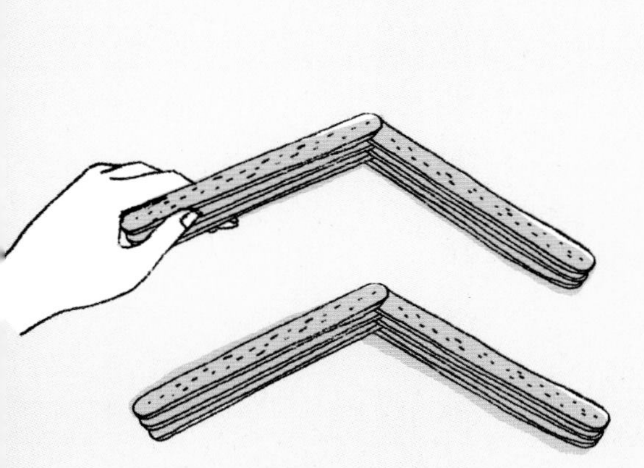

3 Repeat Steps 1 and 2 to build a second bridge for the other side of the ladder.

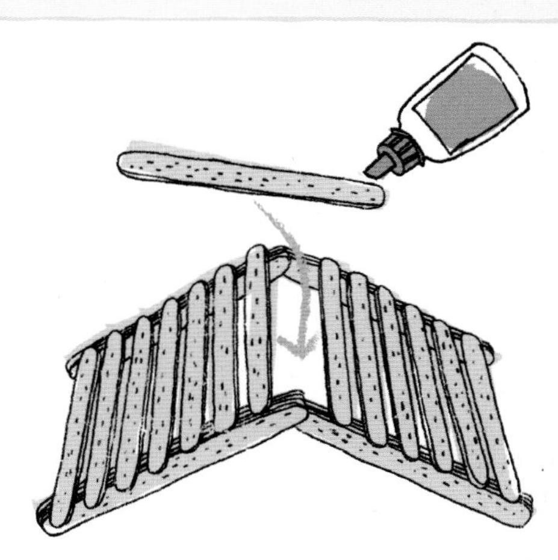

4 Stand the two bridges almost a Popsicle stick length apart and begin to glue sticks in place to act as rungs on a ladder. You will need about seven rungs on each side.

Bar Jump

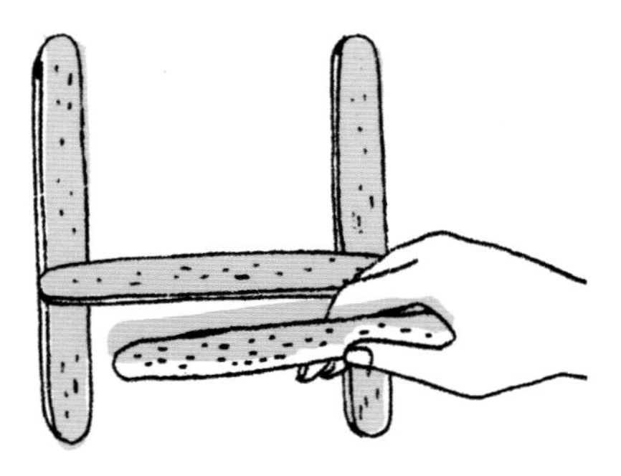

1 Lay out three Popsicle sticks in an "H" shape, placing the crossbar of the "H" on top of the two vertical sticks. Position this crossbar at the height that you think your hammie can climb over. Glue the crossbar in place and add one more crossbar below to make the jump stronger.

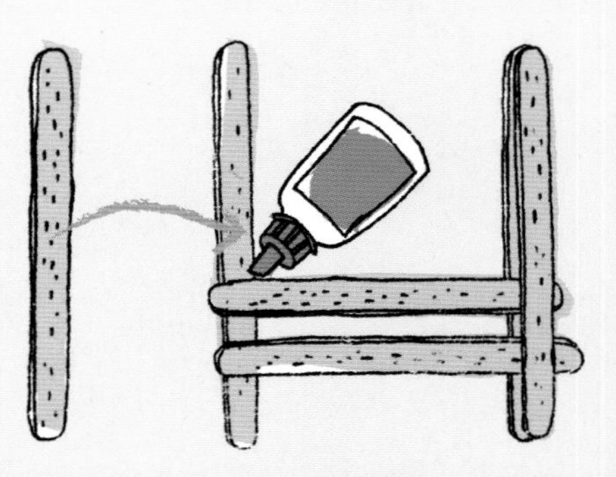

2 Glue one more vertical stick over the top of the crossbars at each side.

3 You can make several bar jumps of different heights for your hamster to try to climb over.

4 To create the base, stand the jump up and glue two sticks horizontally at either side of each vertical leg.

RUNNING THE COURSE

Train your hammie to run the course by guiding him/her through with a treat. After a few trial runs, hammie should get the hang of it.

Seesaw

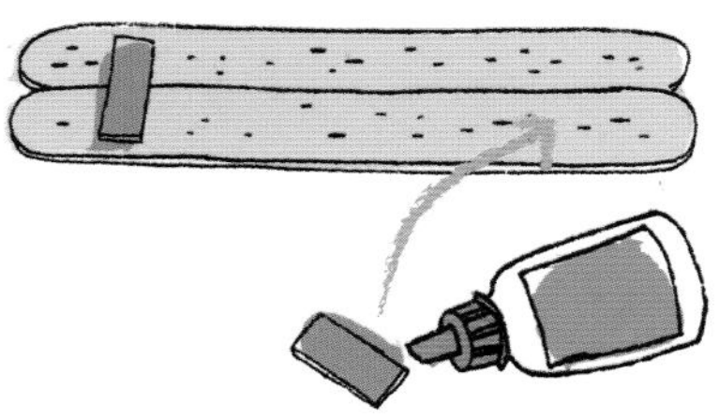

1 Place two jumbo craft sticks side-by-side. Cut two short pieces of Popsicle stick and glue them in place across the craft sticks to make the seesaw plank.

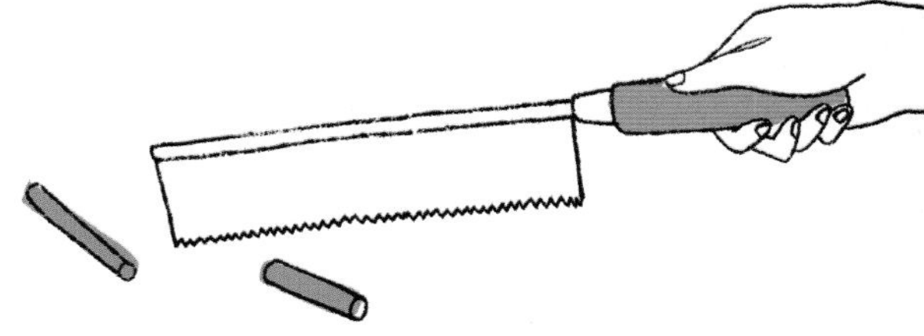

2 Using a small craft saw, carefully cut a piece of wooden dowel that is slightly wider than the wooden plank.

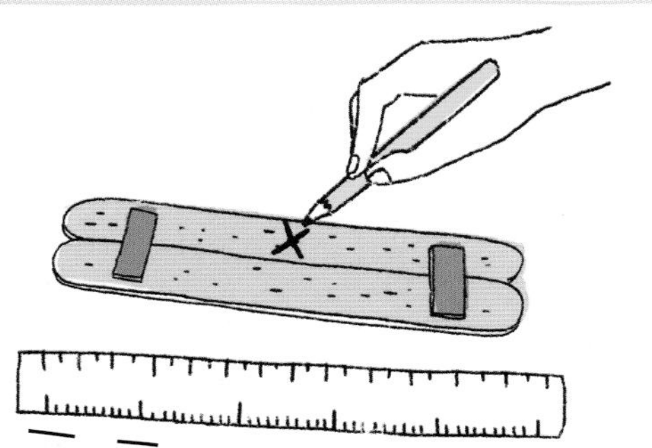

3 Mark the center of the long edge of the plank with a pencil, and glue the dowel in place, just off this center mark. This will ensure that one end of the plank will always be down for your hamster to climb on.

CLIMBING PROJECTS

Hamsters love to climb to survey their environment, so building climbing toys for them will provide a perfect opportunity for promoting healthy exercise and encouraging their curiosity. You'll find lots of ideas to choose from in this section, from a climbing wall to a magical treehouse.

THE SEESAW TUBE

Your hamster thinks it's just a tunnel . . . and then it turns out to be a seesaw! This is a nice little surprise that will have your hammie playing with this project again and again.

TOOLS & MATERIALS

* Toilet paper tube
* Ruler
* Corrugated cardboard
* Pencil
* Scissors
* Bamboo skewers
* Strong, nontoxic glue

OPTIONAL:

* Nontoxic markers or paint

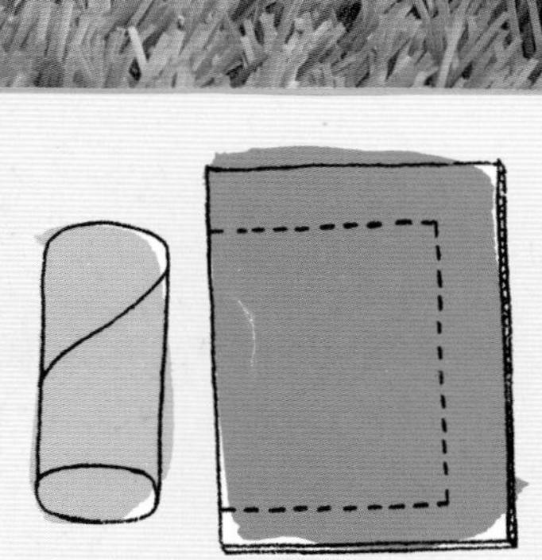

1 Measure your toilet paper tube and then draw a rectangle on the corrugated cardboard that is the same length and twice as wide as this.

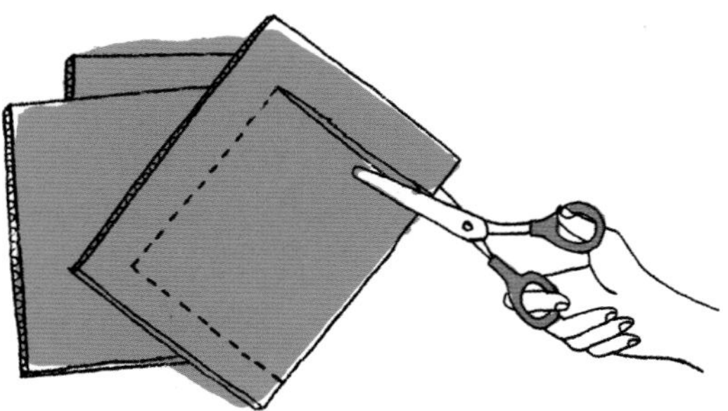

2 Using scissors, cut out this rectangle, then trace and cut two more.

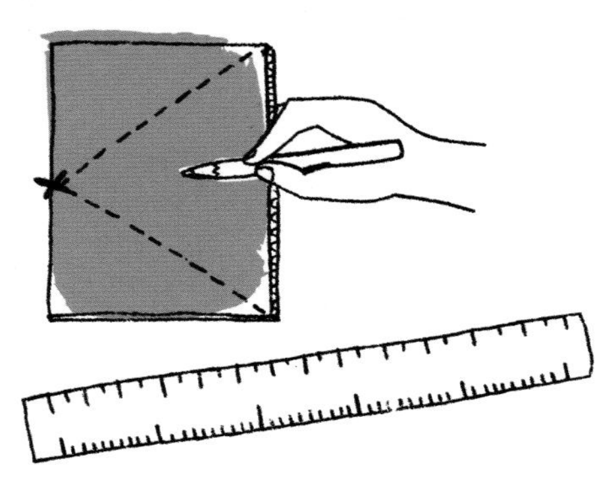

3 On two of the rectangles, make a mark at the center of one of the long sides. Using a ruler, draw a line from this mark to each of the opposite corners to make a triangle. Cut out these large triangles.

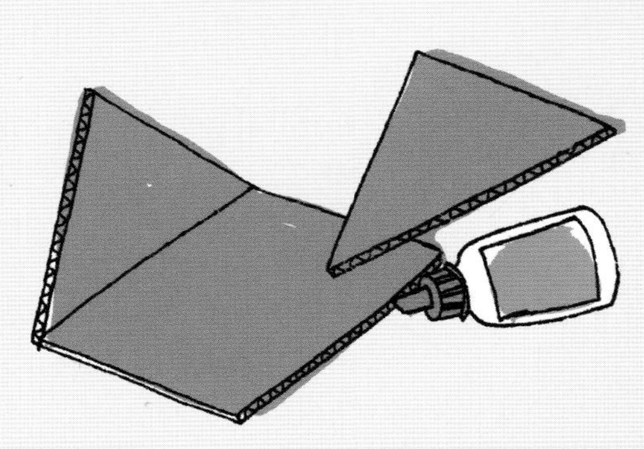

4 Stand each triangle up on its longest side and glue onto the long sides of the rectangle.

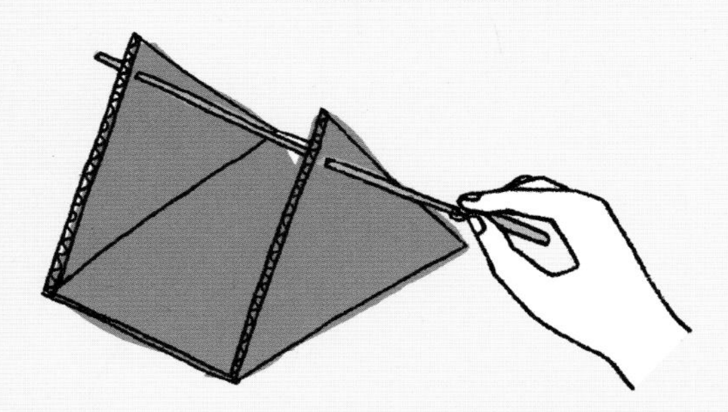

5 Use a bamboo skewer to poke a hole near the top of each triangle. Then remove the skewer.

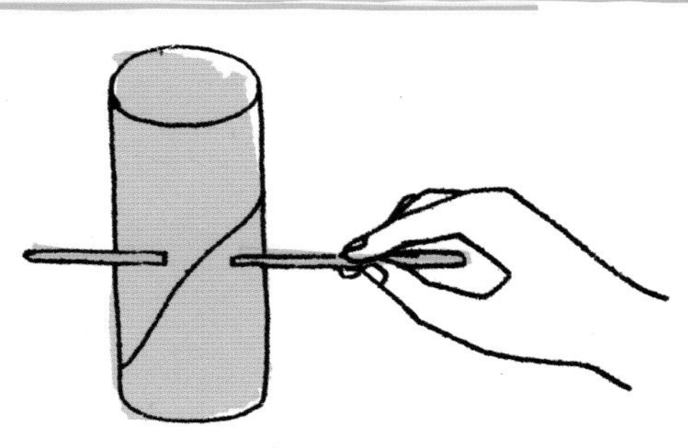

6 Use the skewer to poke two holes side by side, near the center of the toilet paper tube. Remove the skewer.

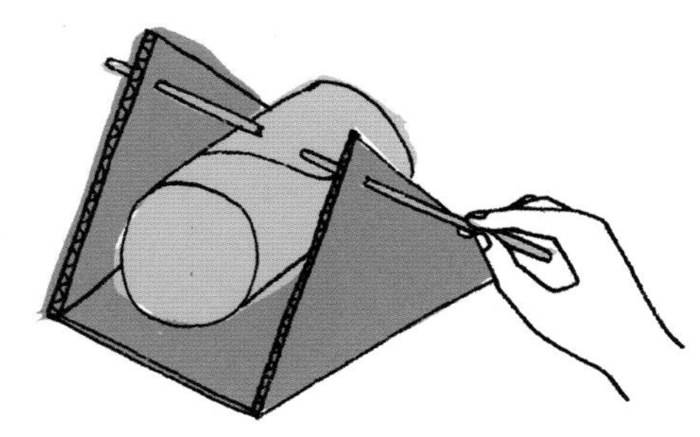

7 Hold the toilet paper tube between the two triangle supports so that all four holes line up. Thread a skewer through the hole in one triangle, the two holes in the tube and then out through the other triangle. Use scissors to trim the ends of the skewer.

THE CLIMBING WALL WITH LADDER

With this project, your hamster has two options — climb straight to the top on the ladder or tackle the extra challenge of the climbing wall!

TOOLS & MATERIALS

* Jumbo craft sticks
* Strong, nontoxic glue
* Scissors
* Bamboo skewers
* String

OPTIONAL:

* Nontoxic markers or paint

MAKE MULTIPLES

Try making two of these climbing walls and attaching them together at the top to make an A-frame for twice the fun!

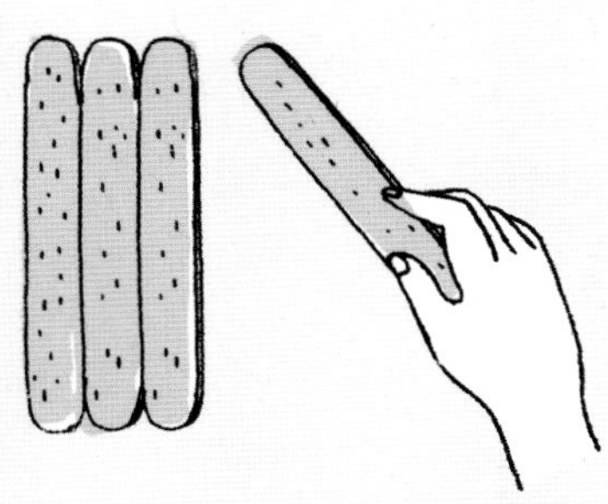

1 Lay four jumbo craft sticks side by side.

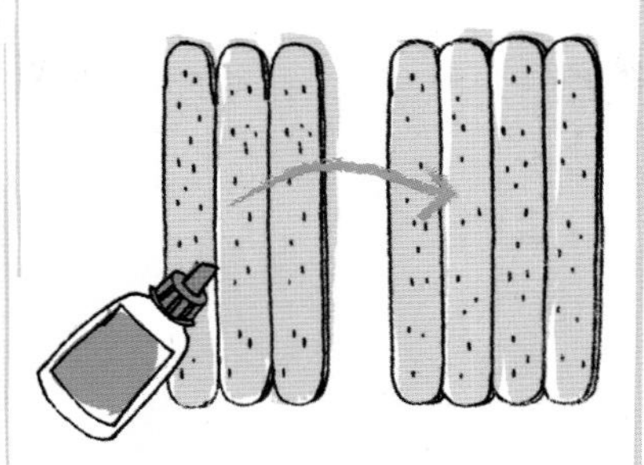

2 Glue three craft sticks over the seams of the original four to make a sturdy wall.

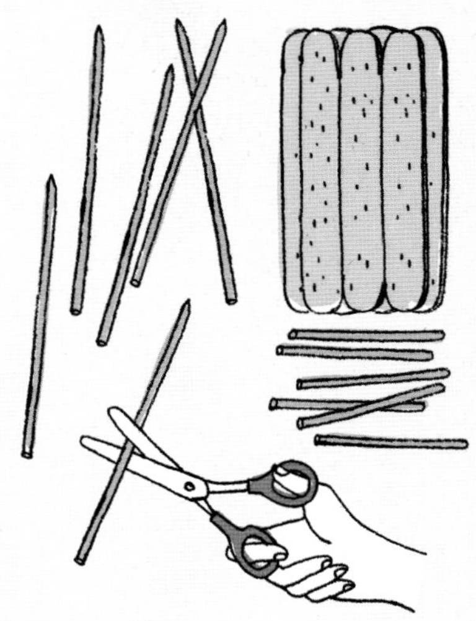

3 Using scissors, cut bamboo skewers into pieces that are the width of the wall. Cut approximately 16 pieces in total.

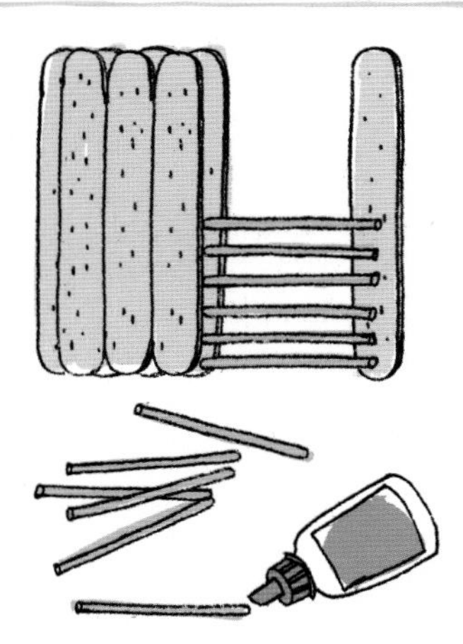

4 Position another craft stick for the outside of the ladder. Glue the bamboo skewer pieces between the wall and this outside stick to make the ladder rungs. Space the rungs far enough apart for your hamster to get his/her feet in between.

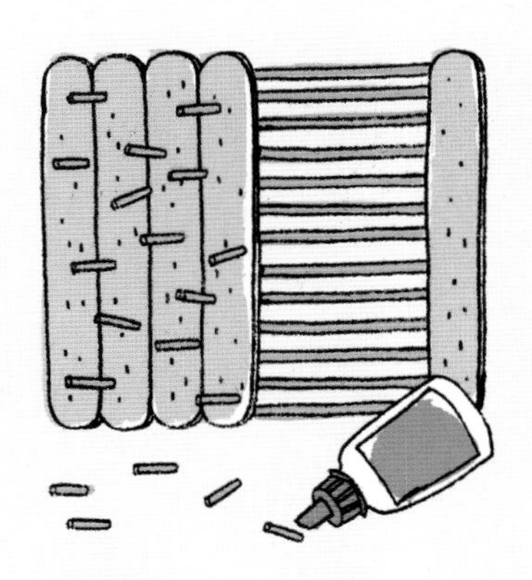

5 Turn the climbing wall over so that the front is facing up. Cut approximately 20 short pieces of bamboo skewer and glue these all over the front of the wall. These will act as footholds for your hamster to use when climbing the wall.

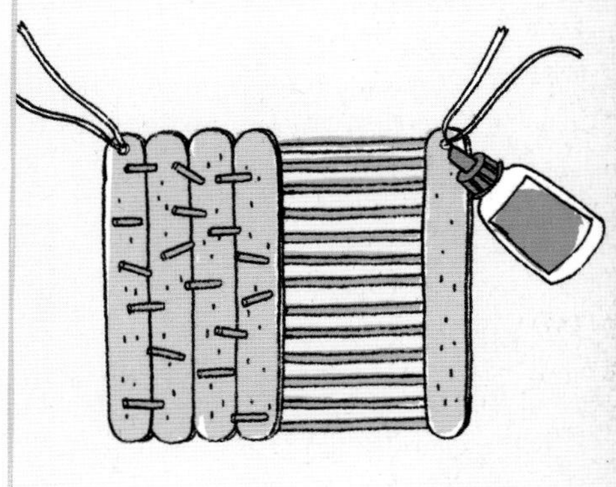

6 Flip the wall back over. Cut two pieces of string a few inches long, fold these in half, and glue one to each top corner of the wall. Lean the climbing wall and ladder against the side of your hamster's cage, using the strings to attach it to the bars of the cage.

THE TREEHOUSE

Imagine how excited your hamster will be when he/she gets an awesome treehouse! There are ladders to climb, different levels to explore, a house to hide in and a swing to play on. Always supervise your hamster when playing.

TOOLS & MATERIALS

* Corrugated cardboard
* Pencil
* Scissors
* Utility knife
* Cutting mat
* Strong, nontoxic glue
* Bamboo skewers
* Sewing needle
* String

OPTIONAL:

* Nontoxic markers or paint and paper

KEEP BUILDING

You can add more to the treehouse such as extra houses or railings on the platforms — or even turn the tree trunk into a climbing wall (see The Climbing Wall with Ladder, pages 40–41).

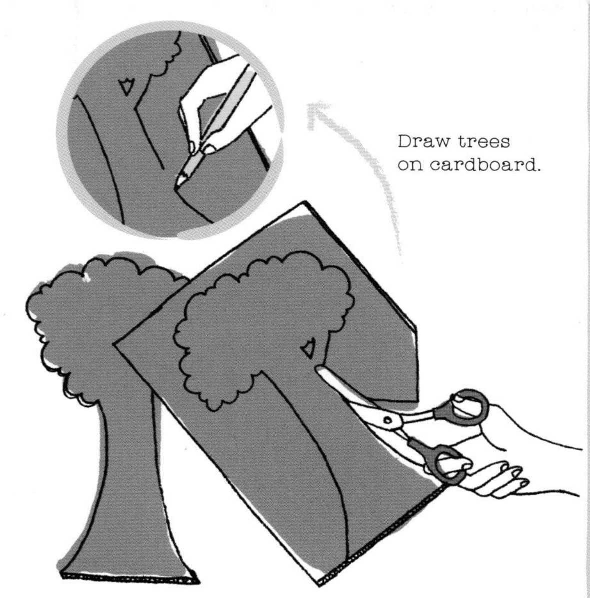

1 On the corrugated cardboard, draw two wide trees of the same height. Make sure that the bases of the trees are wide. Cut these out with scissors.

2 Using a utility knife or scissors, cut a slit in one tree from the middle to the top and then in the other tree from the middle to the bottom. These slits should be the width of the cardboard.

3 Using these slits, slot the two cardboard trees together and glue in place.

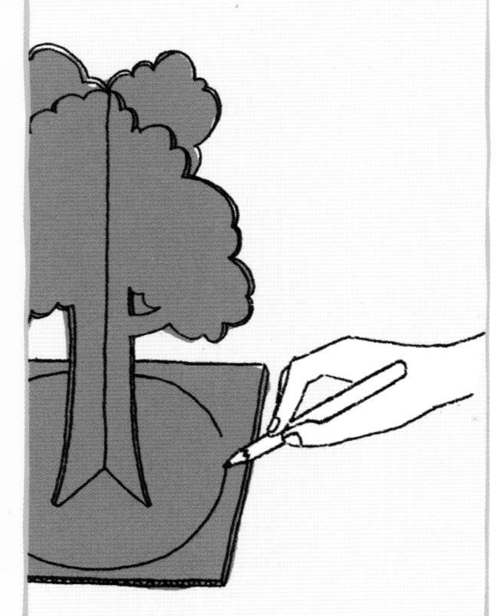

4 Stand the tree on cardboard and draw out a circular base that is as wide as the widest part of your tree.

5 Cut out this base and glue the tree on top.

6 Choose a position near the top of the tree for a house. Cut out a small rectangular platform for the floor of the house.

7 Cut out walls and a roof to match the size of the floor. Don't forget to cut out a door! Glue the house together, then position and glue in place on the tree.

8 Make platforms for the trunk of the tree by cutting three rectangular shapes from the cardboard. Cut a small slit on one side of each rectangle to slot it onto the tree.

9 Fit the platforms onto the tree trunk at different heights, securing in place with glue.

10 Make ladders for each platform level: cut bamboo skewers to the correct height for the upright arms, then cut short pieces of bamboo for the rungs of the ladder. Glue the rungs onto the arms.

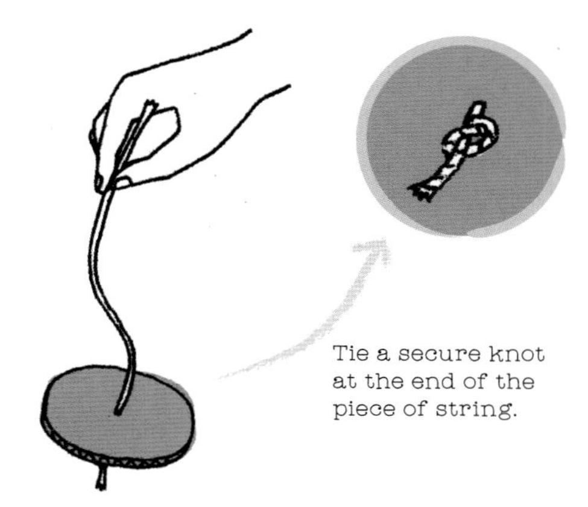

Tie a secure knot at the end of the piece of string.

11 To make a swing, cut a small circle out of cardboard and poke a hole in the center with a needle. Pull a piece of string through the hole and tie a secure knot on the end. Hang the swing from one of the platforms using glue.

12 Decorate your treehouse with markers, nontoxic paint or paper. You might add leaves, bark, fruit, birds, animals or put your hamster's name on the house.

PLATFORM AND RAMP

Climbing is a favorite hamster activity, and once your furry friend reaches the platform, he/she can hang out and survey the domain! Making play areas at different levels for your hamster enriches his/her environment and gives a variety of spaces to choose from.

TOOLS & MATERIALS

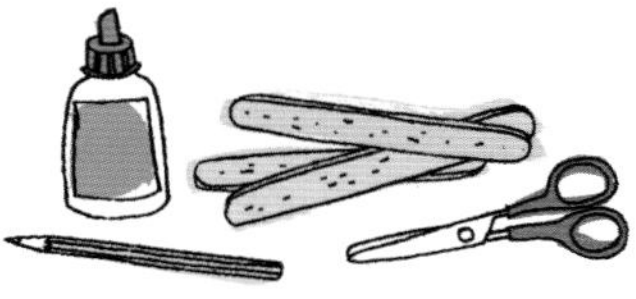

* Popsicle sticks or jumbo craft sticks
* Strong, nontoxic glue
* Pencil
* Scissors

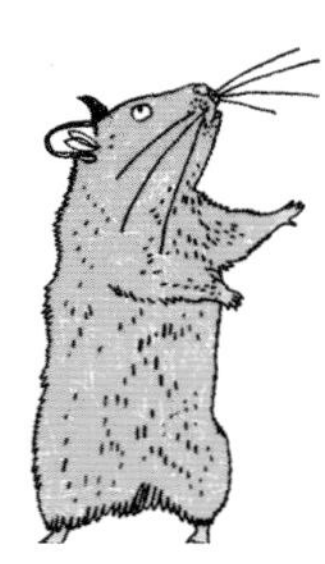

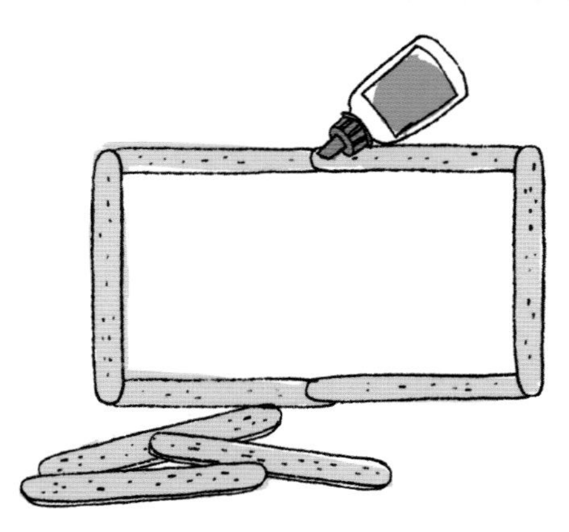

1 Decide how big you want the platform to be by laying out a rectangle of Popsicle sticks (we've used six sticks here). Glue the sticks together to make a frame.

2 Glue more Popsicle sticks side by side across the frame, creating a solid floor.

3 Check that the platform feels sturdy. If you think that it needs to be stronger, flip the platform over and glue cross-pieces of Popsicle sticks in place for extra support.

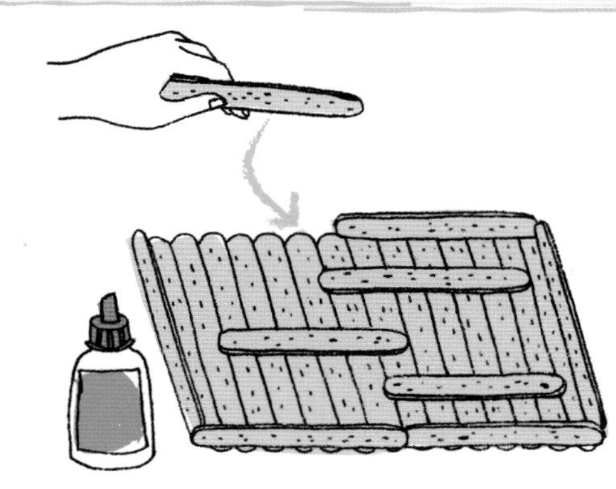

4 On the underside of the platform, glue Popsicle sticks on their edge around the perimeter of the frame.

5 Repeat Step 4 on the top of the platform — this will act as a rim to keep the hamster or any toys from falling off.

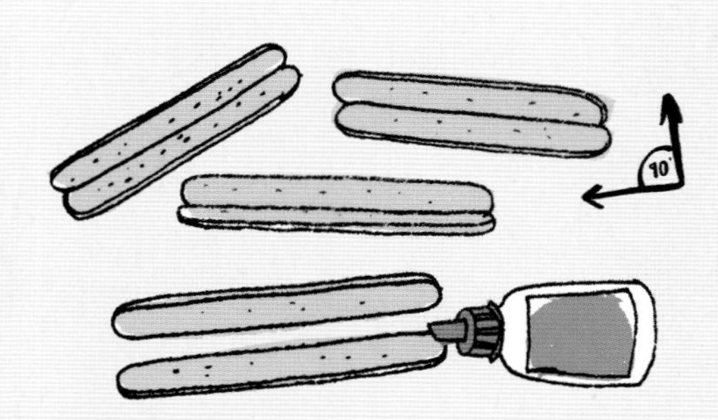

6 Make legs for the platform with four pairs of Popsicle sticks. Glue the long sides of each pair together in a right angle.

7 Turn the platform upside down and glue each leg into a corner of the frame.

8 Lean a pair of Popsicle sticks against the platform to figure out how long the ramp needs to be. Mark the overlap of these sticks with a pencil and glue together at these points. Repeat this for the second arm of the ramp.

CUSTOMIZE THE PLATFORM

You can add more to your platform, such as a fence or hideout. You might also make platforms of different heights and join them together with more ramps to create a multi-level playground for hammie.

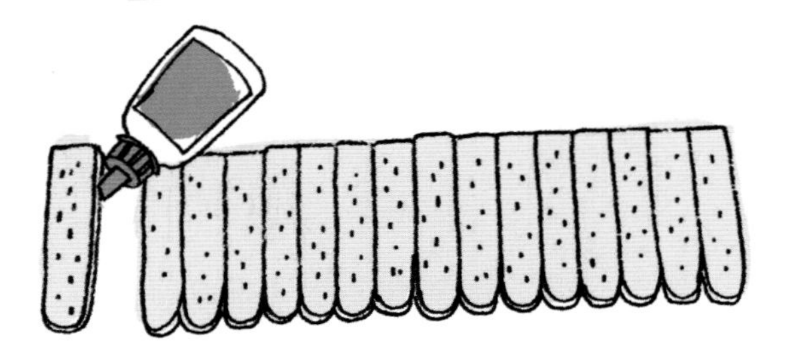

9 Cut a number of Popsicle sticks in half — enough to fill the length of the ramp. Glue these in place across both ramp arms.

10 Using some more cut Popsicle sticks, add treads to the front of the ramp to make it easier to climb.

FENCING IT OFF

Add a fence barrier around the platform for some extra security. This can easily be made with pieces of Popsicle sticks and then glued to the edge of the platform.

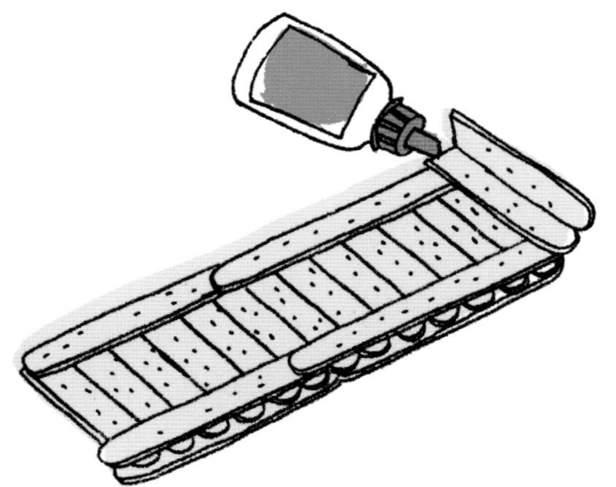

11 Glue a pair of cut sticks together at a right angle and stick to the top edge of the back of the ramp to form a tab that will hook over the rim of the platform.

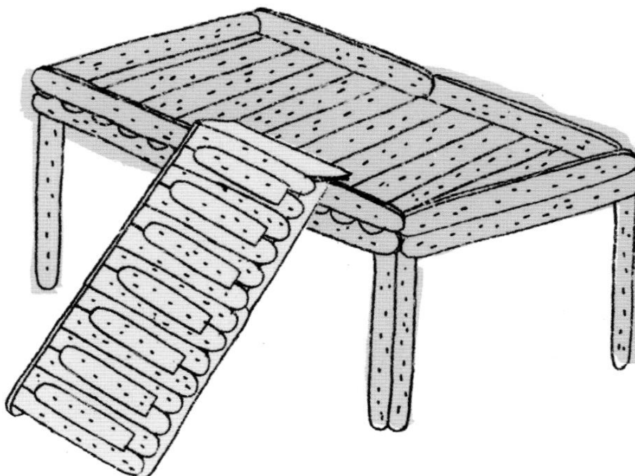

12 Attach the ramp to the platform, hooking it over the rim.

THE SWING

Make your hamster's cage feel like a playground by adding this simple and exciting swing.

CHEWING ISSUES

If your hamster tends to chew through string, you can replace it with wire.

TOOLS & MATERIALS

* Popsicle sticks
* Strong, nontoxic glue
* Scissors
* String

1 Start by making a support for the swing: glue three Popsicle sticks together in a triangle formation, then glue another stick onto the bottom of the triangle. Repeat this to make two triangles.

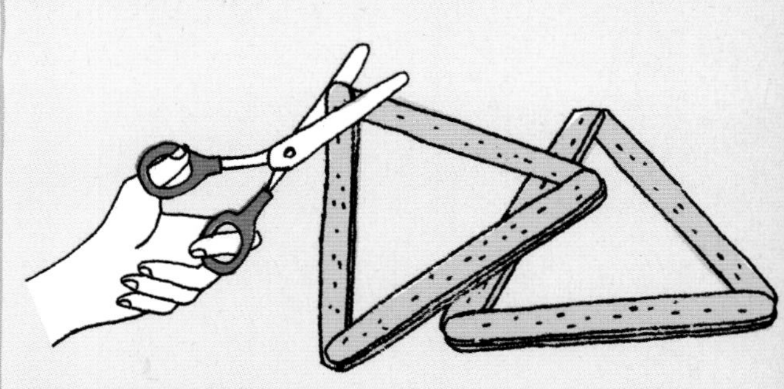

2 Using scissors, trim the rounded edges from only the top of the triangles to make them flat.

3 Glue four Popsicle sticks together to make a square base. With the doubled side down, glue one triangle onto one side of the square base. Glue the second triangle to the opposite side of the base.

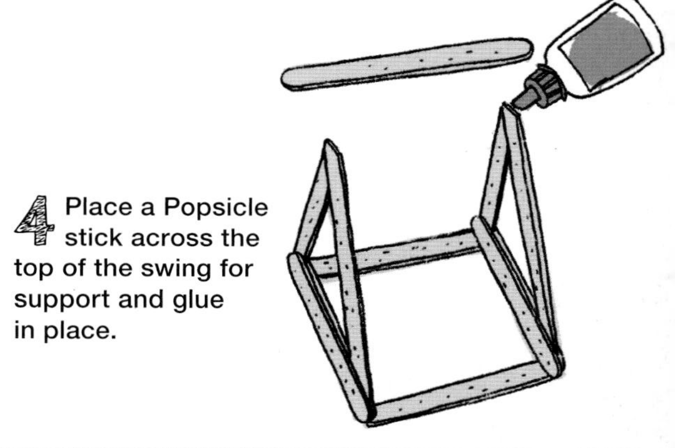

4 Place a Popsicle stick across the top of the swing for support and glue in place.

5 To make the swing platform, lay out eight sticks side by side. Make sure that the platform is narrow enough to easily fit inside the swing frame. Trim three pieces of Popsicle stick for cross-pieces and glue onto the bottom of the platform.

6 Wrap a piece of string around both sides of the platform and loop each one over the top bar of the swing. Tie each piece of string in a knot to suspend the platform.

THE BENDY BRIDGE

This bridge will help your hamster get from one place to another, with the added challenge of hills and bends. You can use wooden dowels for this, or sticks for a more natural look.

MULTI-PURPOSE

Your bendy bridge can be used as a ramp, a bridge to connect two platforms or as a toy all on its own.

TOOLS & MATERIALS

* Wooden dowels (you can also use sticks from outside but make sure you choose a safe type of wood and disinfect according to the directions on page 11)
* Small craft saw
* Sandpaper
* Pencil
* Drill and drill bit
* Wire
* Wire cutters
* Pliers

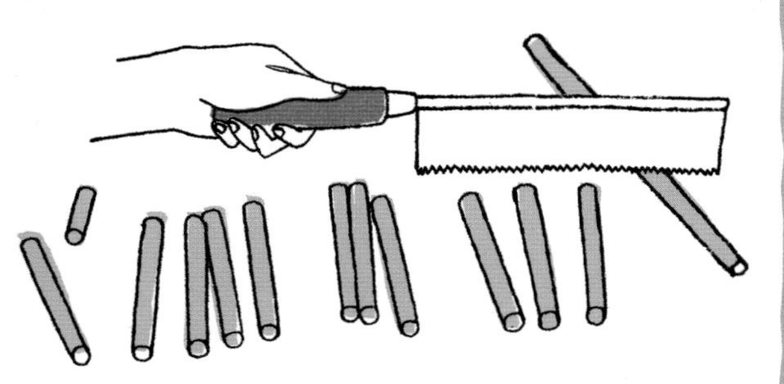

1 Decide on the width of your bridge and, using a saw, cut a number of dowels or sticks to this width. The number of dowels you use can vary depending on the length of your bridge. Supervise children throughout when making this project.

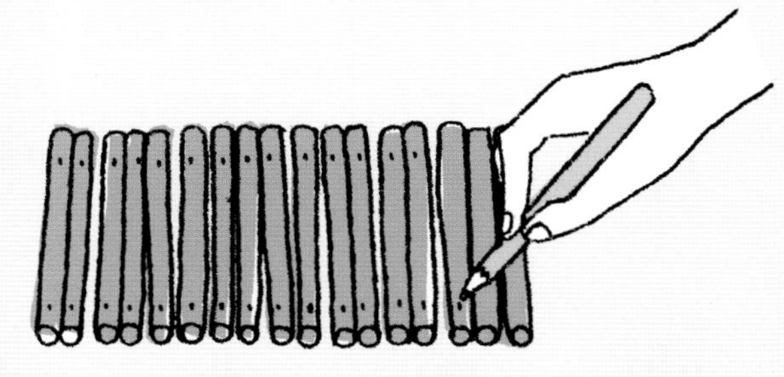

2 Sand any rough edges on the dowels and then line them all up. Use a pencil to mark the holes for threading the two wire pieces, approximately ½ in. (1 cm) from each edge.

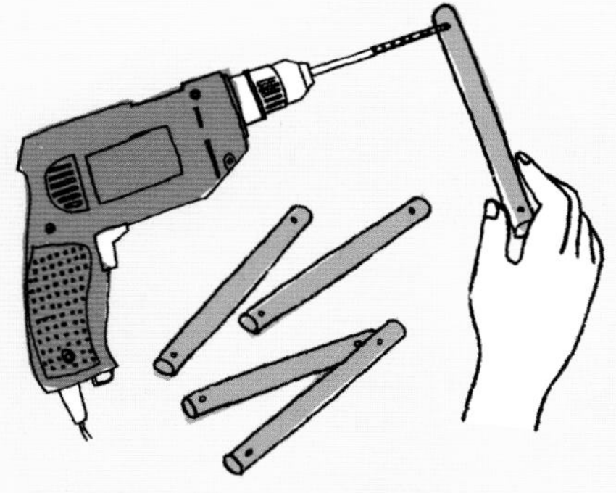

3 Using a drill, carefully make the holes in each dowel at the marked points.

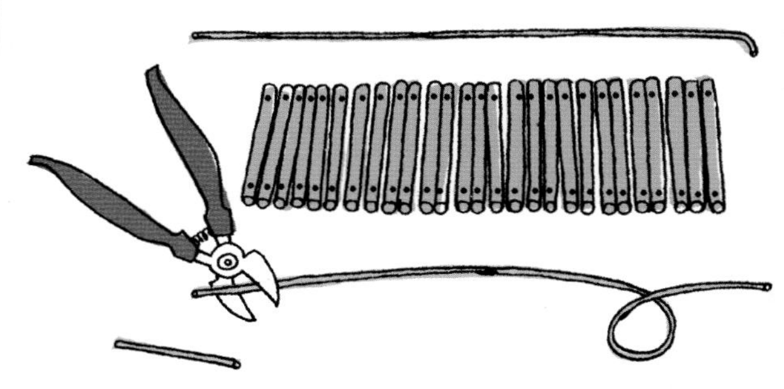

4 Cut two pieces of wire that are slightly longer than the bridge will be. Bend over one end of each piece of wire to prevent the dowels from sliding off.

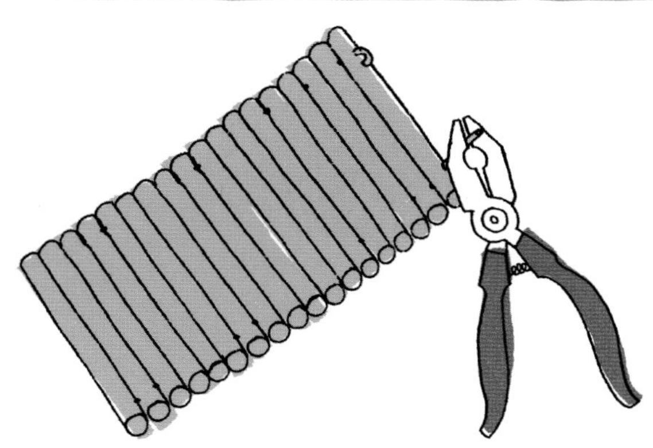

5 Thread each of the dowels onto the two pieces of wire. Once all the dowels are in place, trim the ends of the wires, leaving ½ in. (1 cm) or so. Bend these ends over, making sure to tuck in any sharp edges.

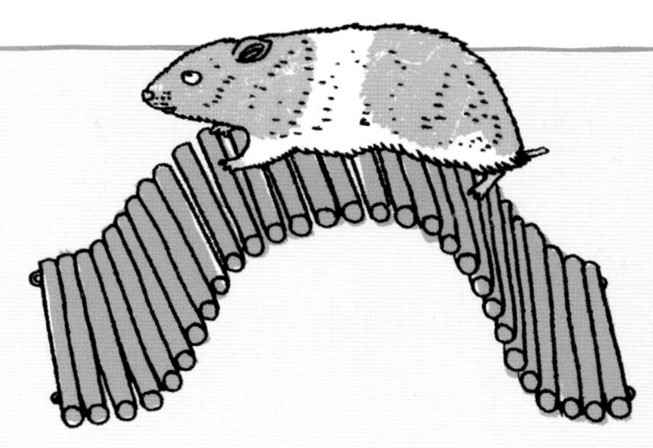

6 The wire will allow the bridge to hold its form, so bend it into a fun, hilly shape and let your hamster enjoy!

DIGGING PROJECTS

Digging is a popular activity for hamsters as they would be used to foraging for food and digging small tunnels in their natural environment. Choose from projects such as the Sand Bath or Miniature Landscape with Digging Pit in this section, to keep your hamster busy and active.

THE SAND BATH

Many hamsters will enjoy digging and rolling around in this sand bath. The sand helps to keep their fur clean and in good condition.

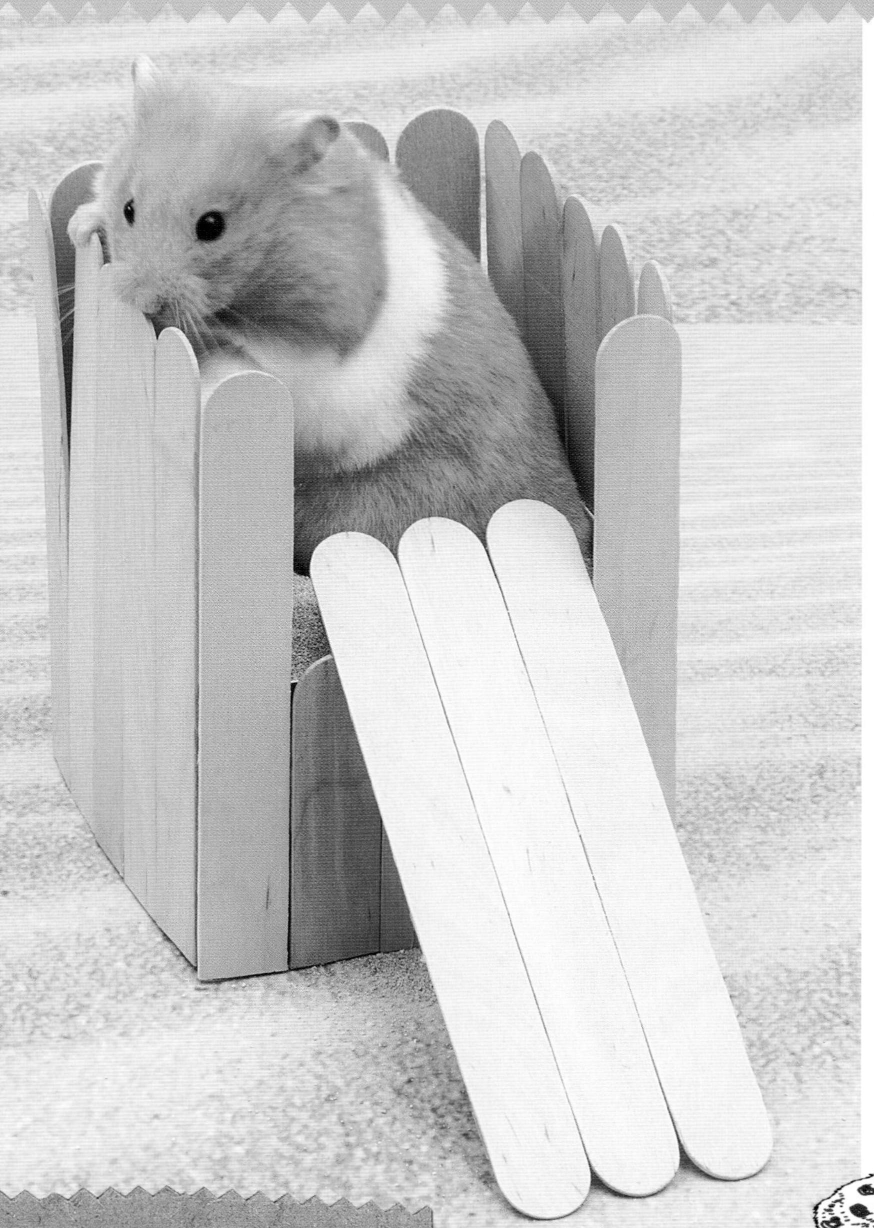

TOOLS & MATERIALS

* Milk carton (half gallon size)
* Jumbo craft sticks
* Popsicle sticks
* Safe, nontoxic glue
* Scissors
* Sand — use chinchilla bath sand (not dust or powder)

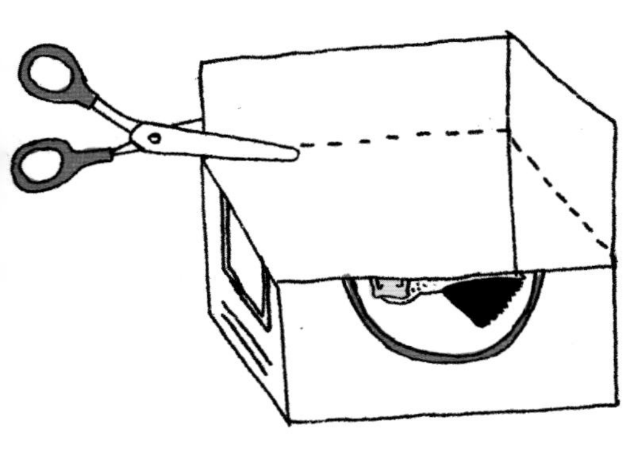

1 Using scissors, cut off the bottom section of the milk carton so that you are left with a box approximately 3 in. (7.5 cm) high.

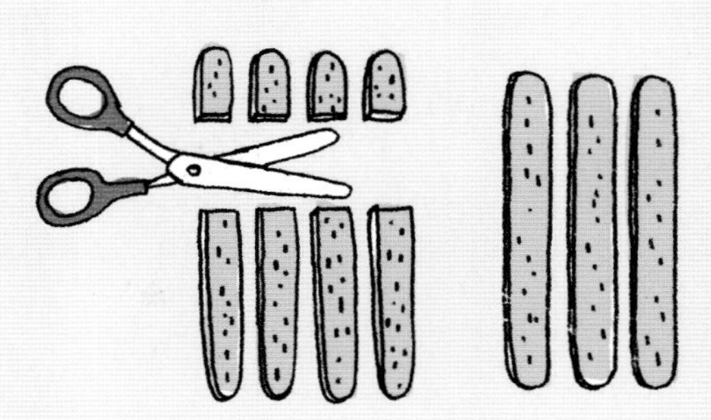

2 Using scissors, carefully trim one end of a bunch of jumbo craft sticks or Popsicle sticks to leave a flat edge. You'll need enough to go around three sides of your milk carton box — here, we've used 17 jumbo craft sticks.

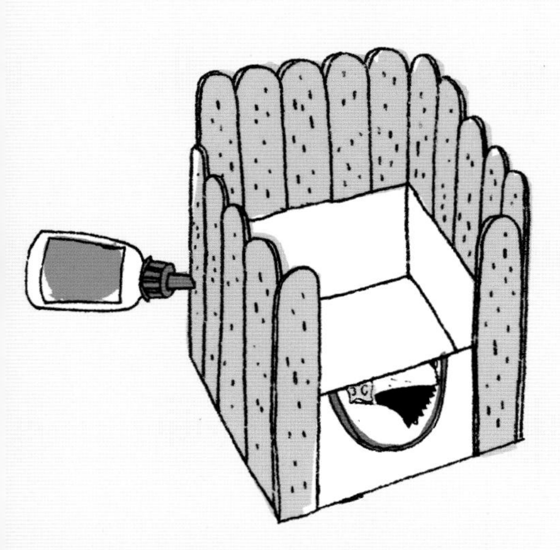

3 Glue the sticks side-by-side around three sides of the box, making sure that the rounded parts point upward. Place one stick at either edge of the fourth side.

4 Carefully trim approximately three craft sticks to the same height as the box. Glue these onto the remaining space on the fourth side, again with the rounded ends pointing upward.

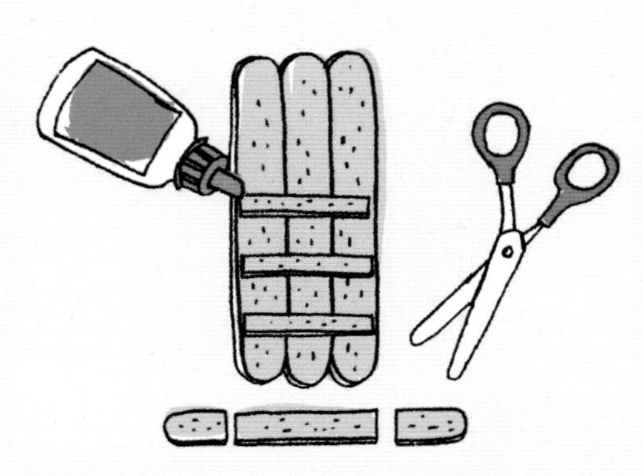

5 Make a ramp by placing three craft sticks side by side. Trim Popsicle sticks to the width of the ramp, and glue them on, leaving spaces in between.

6 Position the ramp on the short side of the bath, so that your hamster can easily climb up. Finally, pour a couple of inches of sand into the box.

DIGGING FOR TREATS

Try hiding treats in the sand to encourage your hamster to dig.

MINIATURE LANDSCAPE WITH DIGGING PIT

You can set the scene for a hamster adventure with this fun project! Make a tiny landscape that has a sand pit to dig in, as well as a hill to climb and a tunnel to run through.

TOOLS & MATERIALS

* Corrugated cardboard
* Some small cardboard boxes — used tissue boxes are great for this (make sure that any ink is soy- or vegetable-based)
* Toilet paper tubes
* Newspapers (make sure the ink is soy- or vegetable-based)
* White copy paper
* Sand — you can use chinchilla bath sand (not dust or powder)
* Papier mâché paste (see instructions on page 11)
* Scissors
* Ruler
* Nontoxic glue

OPTIONAL:

* Nontoxic paint
* Paintbrush

1 Start by making a base. Using a ruler and scissors, cut the corrugated cardboard to the size that you want your landscape to be. (Here, our base is 17 x 12 in./43 x 30 cm.)

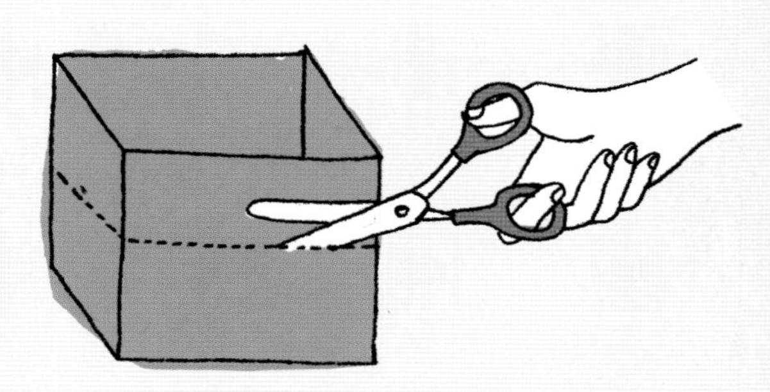

2 To make the sides of the sand pit, cut down one of the small cardboard boxes to a height of approximately 2½ in. (6.5 cm).

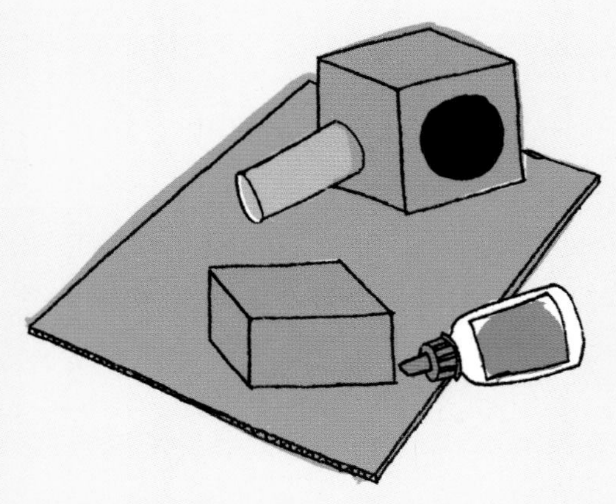

3 Arrange the boxes and toilet paper tubes on your cardboard base to form the shapes for the hills and tunnels of your landscape. Stick these onto the cardboard base using nontoxic glue.

4 Fill in any empty space on the base or make more rounded shapes with balls of crumpled newspaper.

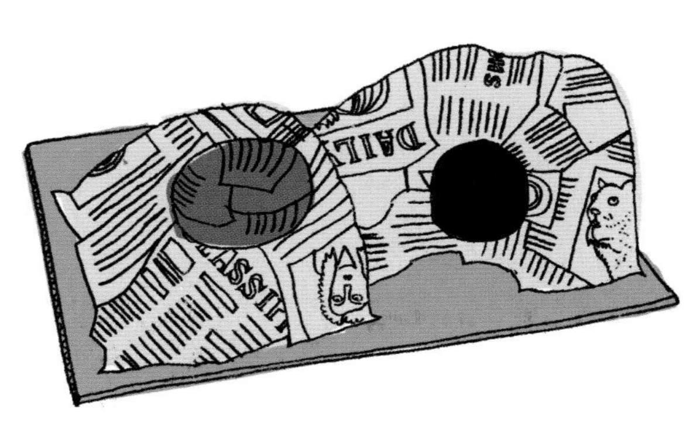

5 Cover all of the shapes you've created with more pieces of newspaper to hold everything in place. Use some tape to hold it together but, if your hamster likes to chew, be sure to remove the tape when you add the papier mâché.

6 Make your papier mâché paste (see page 11). While you are waiting for this to cool, tear some more of the newspaper into strips.

7 Dip strips of newspaper into the paste and apply a layer over your whole landscape.

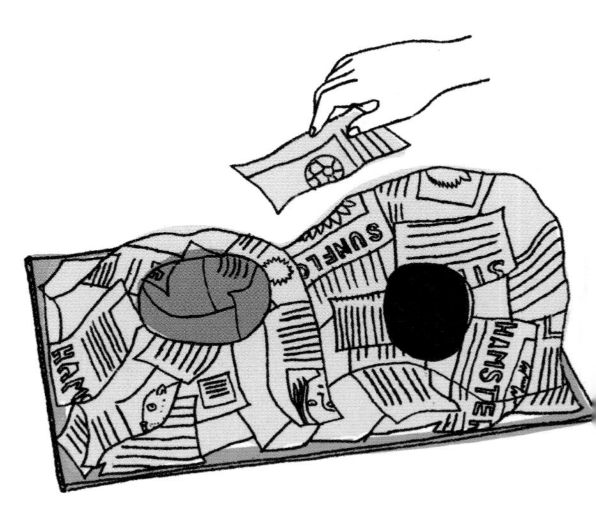

8 Apply three layers of newspaper to the landscape, letting each layer dry before starting the next.

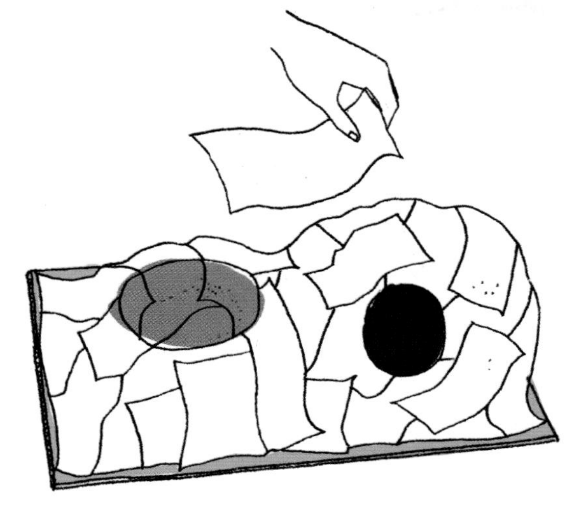

9 Tear the white copy paper into strips, and, using the papier mâché paste, apply a final layer over the landscape.

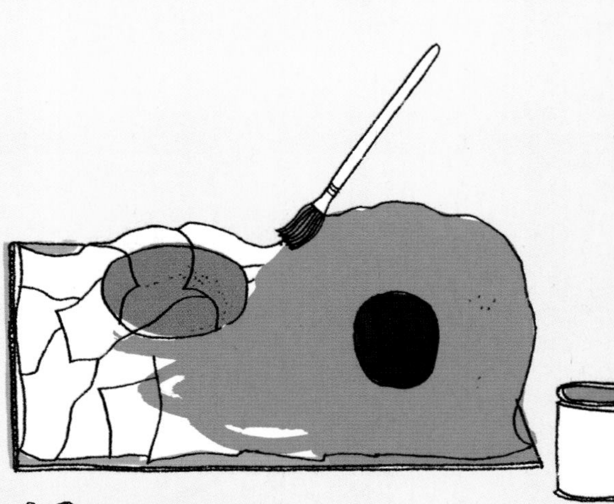

10 Once this last layer is dry, you can paint your landscape using nontoxic paints, if you wish.

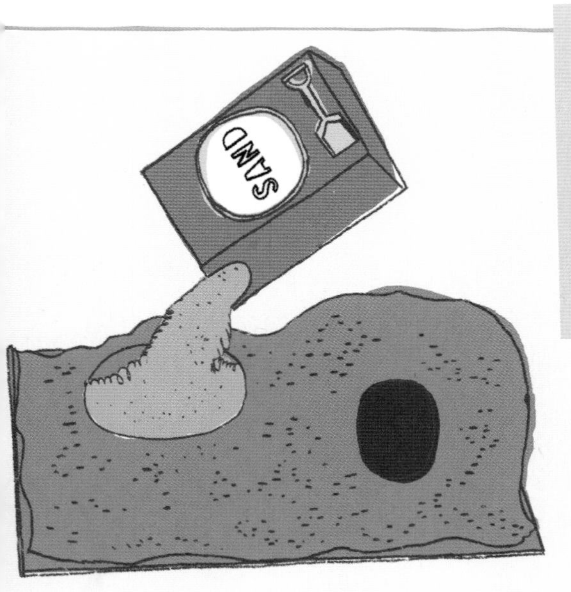

11 Finally, add sand to the digging pit.

ADDITIONAL SHAPES

Try expanding or changing your landscape by creating more rectangular sections and putting them together in different arrangements.

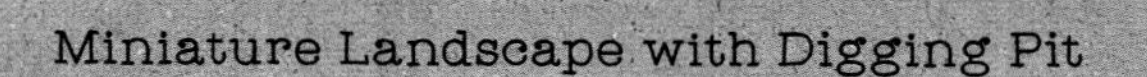

THE DIGGING TOWER

Your hamster will be able to do some serious digging in this tower! Be sure to keep an eye on your hamster while playing with this and don't leave him/her unsupervised.

TOOLS & MATERIALS

* Corrugated cardboard
* Clear plastic food package (a large salad greens box works well)
* Jumbo craft sticks
* Popsicle sticks
* Pencil
* Ruler
* Scissors
* Clear tape
* Strong, nontoxic glue

1 To create the walls of the tower, cut out four rectangles approximately 10 x 7 in. (25 x 18 cm) in size from the corrugated cardboard. You can adjust the size depending on the size of your hamster.

Shredded toilet paper provides a soft base for play.

2 On one wall, cut out an oblong shape for a door. Make sure that it isn't too big, but it needs to be big enough for your hammie to fit through easily.

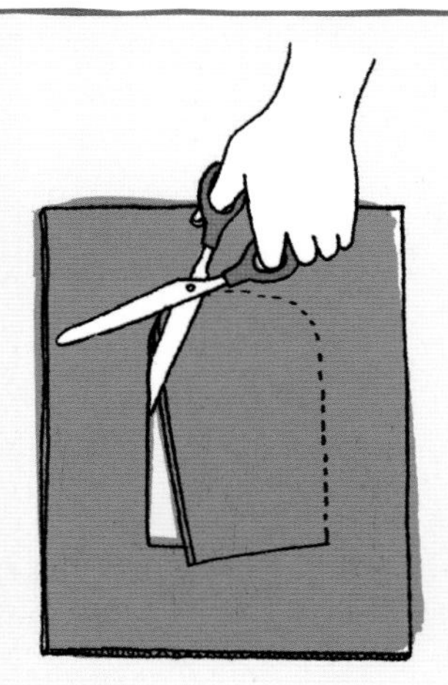

3 On two of the other walls, cut out rectangular holes with one curved edge to act as windows.

4 Using the clear plastic food container, cut two similar-shaped pieces that are slightly larger to cover the windows. Tape these in place, making sure to sand down or cover any rough edges.

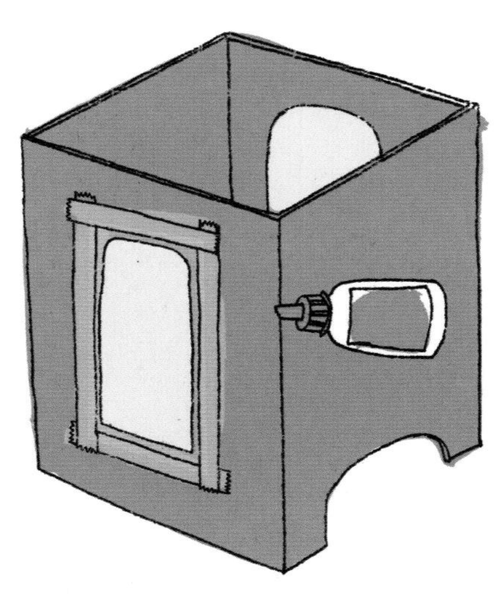

5 Glue or tape the four walls together, with the windows on opposite sides. Make sure that any tape is on the outside of the box — you don't want your hamster to chew on it.

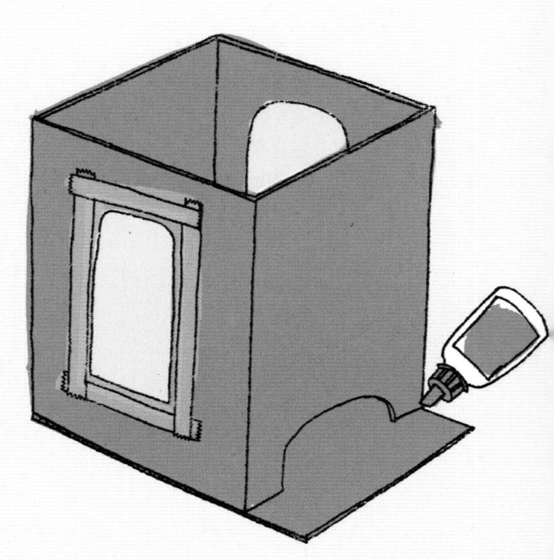

6 Cut out a piece of cardboard for the floor of the tower, which extends a few inches in front of the door. Stick the walls down onto the floor using nontoxic glue.

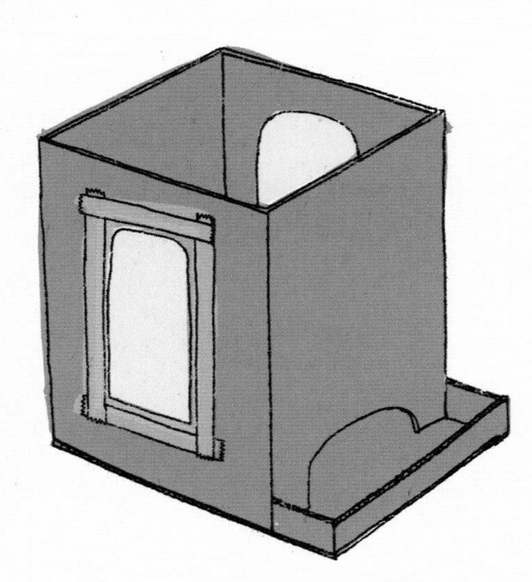

7 Cut out some small strips of cardboard and add these as short walls around the floor, in front of the doorway. This makes a front porch that will catch any bedding that spills out through the door.

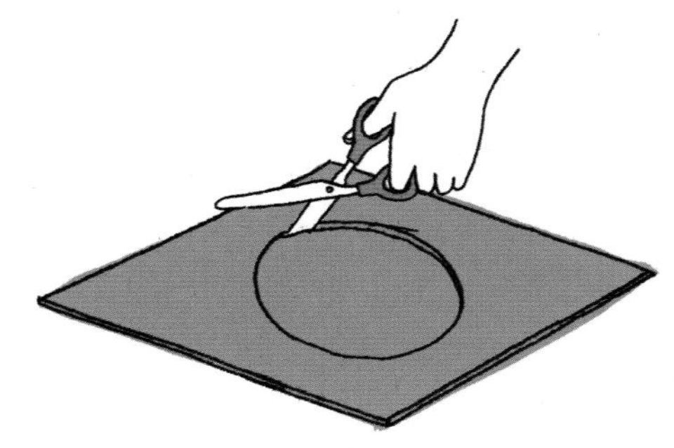

8 To make a lid, cut out a piece of cardboard just a tiny bit bigger than the top opening of the tower. In the middle of this piece, cut a hole large enough for your hamster to climb through easily.

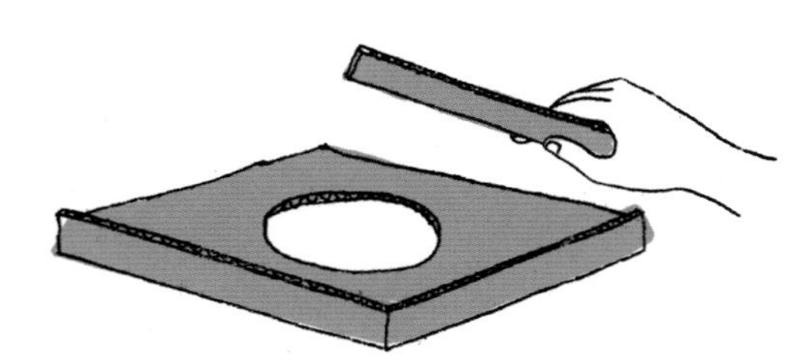

9 Cut four narrow rectangular strips of cardboard to fit around the edge of the lid as a rim. Glue in place.

10 Make a ladder so that your hamster can climb to the top of the tower. Glue together jumbo craft sticks end-to-end for the rails of the ladder — here, we've used three sticks each side, but you can make the ladder longer or shorter to fit the height of your tower. Cut Popsicle sticks into small pieces for the rungs of the ladder, and glue into place across the jumbo craft sticks.

ENCOURAGING TREATS

Show your hamster how to use his/her new toy — hide a tasty treat in the bedding, and then set your hamster on the top of the tower so that he/she can dig in to find it.

11 Fill the tower with shredded toilet paper or bedding.

CHEWING PROJECTS

Hamsters' teeth require special care and attention because they grow continuously throughout their lifetime. Without things for your hamster to chew on, his/her teeth can become damaged or cause injury. In this section, you'll find ideas for a number of different chewing toys that are essential for keeping your pet healthy.

WALNUT SHELL CHEWING TOY

Use empty walnut shells to create a toy that will give your hamster a whole string of reasons to chew, and to keep his/her teeth in shape.

TOOLS & MATERIALS

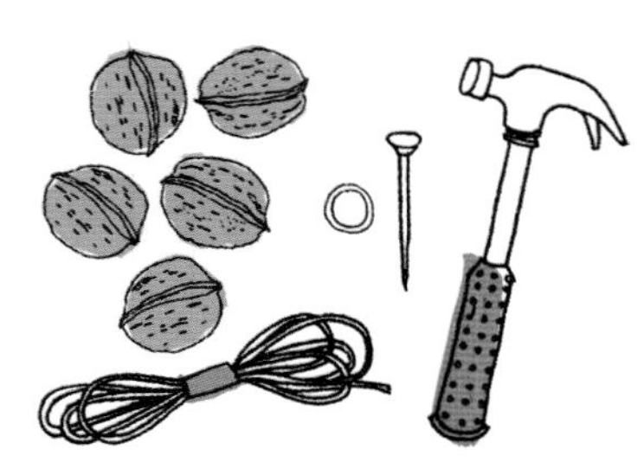

* Walnuts in the shell (you will need at least 5 or 6)
* String (approximately 2 ft./60 cm long)
* Metal washer
* Hammer
* Nail

EASY OPTION

A whole walnut in the shell can also be hours of fun for your hamster as he/she rolls it around and tries to open it.

1 Using the nail, find the weakest point in the join of a walnut shell — this is usually at the head of the walnut. Force the nail in, and wiggle it until the shell cracks down the middle. Crack all the shells open in this way.

2 Remove all of the walnuts from the shells. You can eat them or give them to your hamster as a treat!

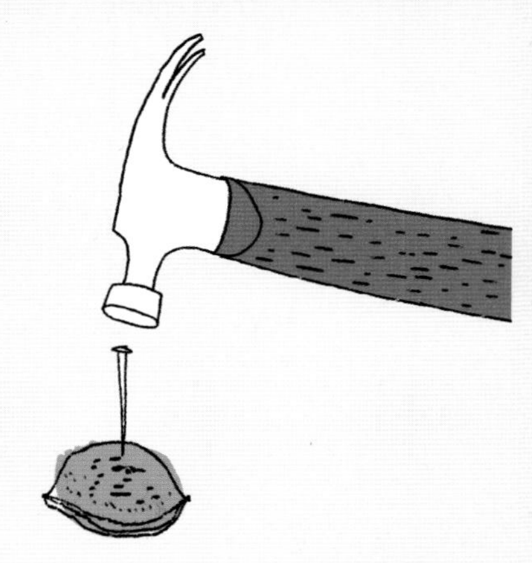

3 Using the hammer and nail, carefully make a small hole in the middle of each walnut shell (or use a drill if you have one). Place each walnut shell open-side down to do this.

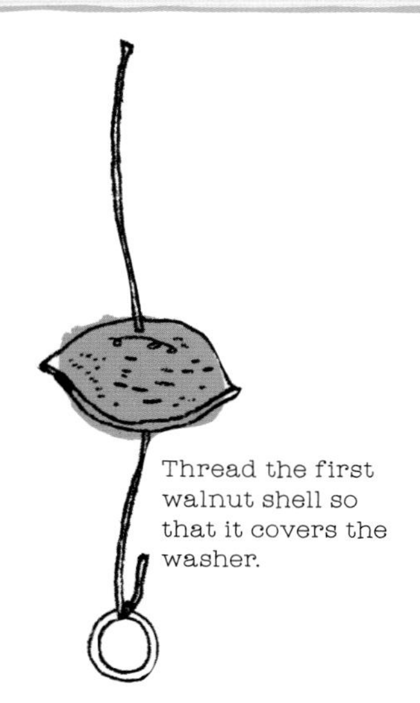

Thread the first walnut shell so that it covers the washer.

4 Securely tie one end of the string onto the metal washer. Thread one walnut shell onto the string, open-side down so that the shell covers the washer.

5 Continue to thread more shells onto the string, open-side up so that each shell makes a bowl. Add as many shells as you like.

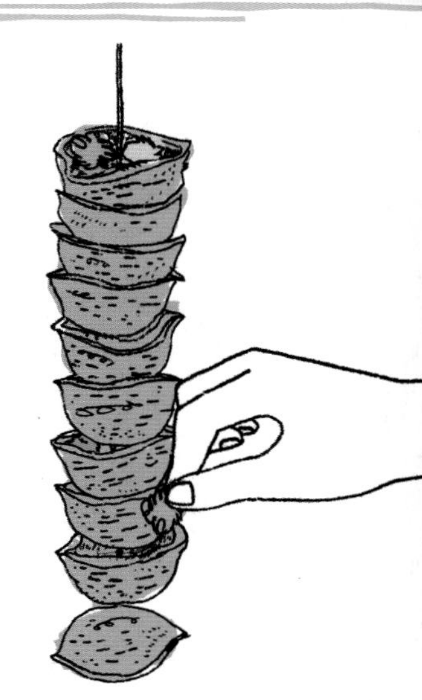

6 When you have reached your desired length, tie the end of the string to the top of your hamster's cage. Tuck some treats inside the shells to encourage your hammie to chew.

TREAT TUBES

Here, you'll find three different ideas for treat tubes that you can make out of toilet paper rolls. Try making all of them, and see which one your hamster likes best.

TOOLS & MATERIALS

* Toilet paper rolls (you'll need 6 to create all 3 versions)
* Sheet of white copy paper or colored paper, made using soy- or vegetable-based inks
* Hamster treats
* Scissors

HEALTHY SNACKS

You don't want your hamster to overeat treats so, if he/she really loves these treat tubes, try replacing some of the treats with food pellets instead.

VERSION 1

VERSION 2

VERSION 3

Version 1

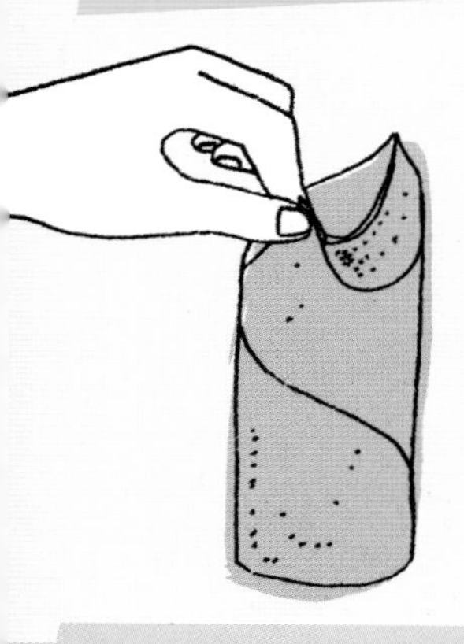

1 The first treat tube is the simplest to make. Take a toilet roll and, on one end, fold in both sides to close it.

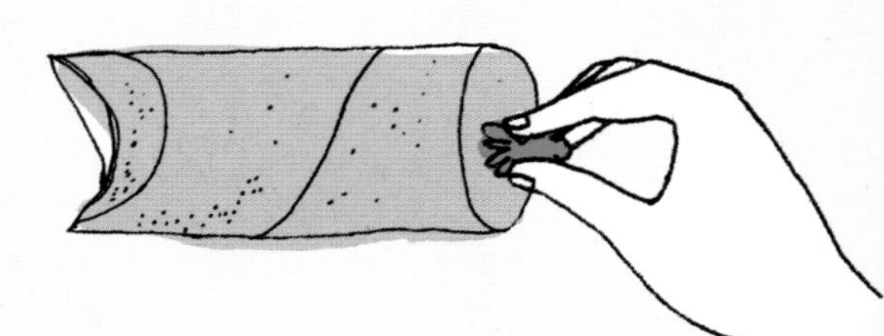

2 Place a couple of treats inside the tube, and then fold the remaining side closed.

Version 2

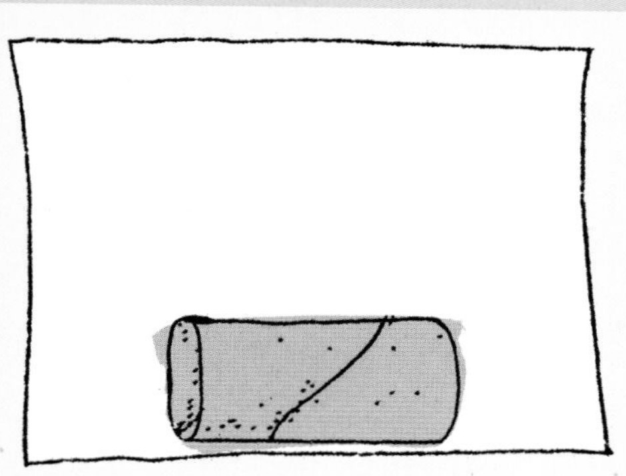

1 For the second treat tube, lay a cardboard tube along the long side of a piece of white copy paper.

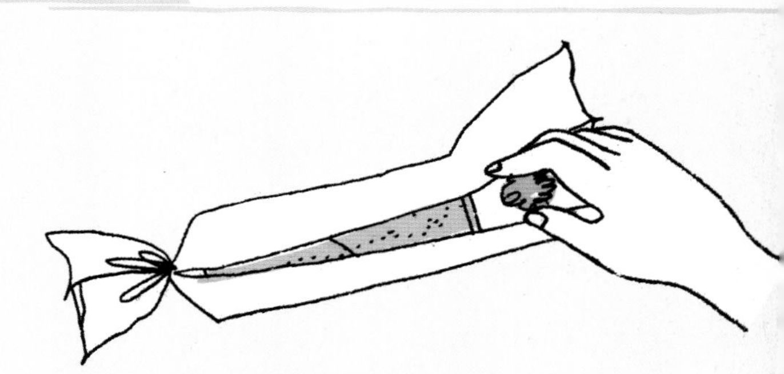

2 Roll the tube up in the paper, and twist one end of the paper closed. Add treats to the middle of the tube, and then twist the paper on the opposite end closed. Trim the ends of the paper if it's too long.

Version 3

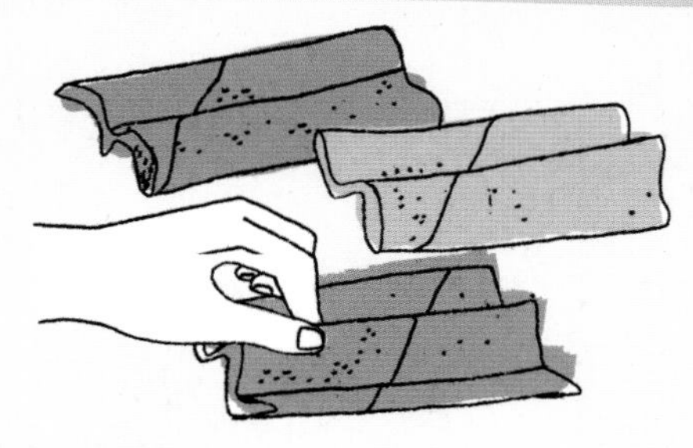

1 You'll need four toilet paper tubes for this version. Take three of the tubes, squash them flat, and concertina them along the long sides.

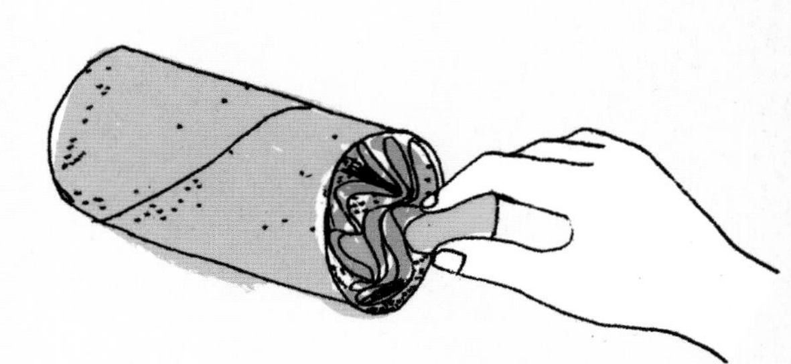

2 Push the three crumpled tubes into the remaining tube, and then push treats into the gaps between the cardboard at the ends.

TREAT BALL

This is an easy-to-make toy that is fun for your hamster to roll, play with and chew. Inside the ball, you can hide food pellets, treats or even healthy vegetables.

TOOLS & MATERIALS

* Toilet paper rolls (you'll need one for each ball that you want to make)
* Food pellets, treats or small pieces of vegetables
* Scissors

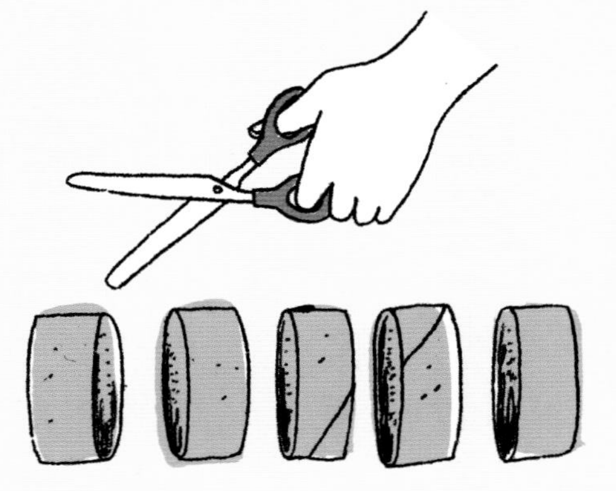

1 Using scissors, cut a toilet paper tube into five equal pieces.

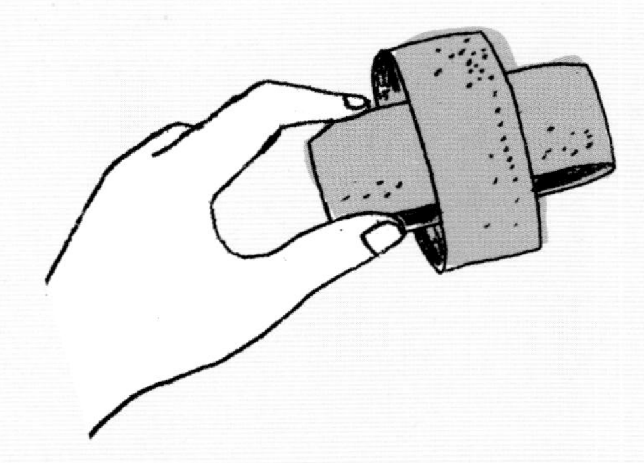

2 Position one piece of cardboard inside another so that they form an X-shape.

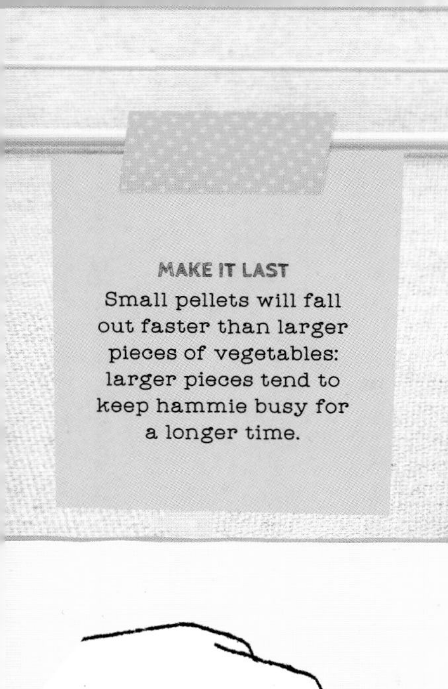

MAKE IT LAST

Small pellets will fall out faster than larger pieces of vegetables: larger pieces tend to keep hammie busy for a longer time.

3 Put a third piece around the outside of the other two so that it holds them together.

4 Insert a food pellet, a treat or a piece of vegetable into the middle of the cardboard formation.

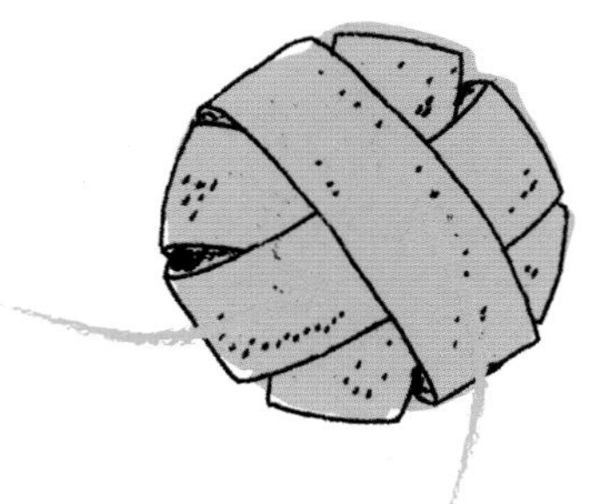

5 Position the remaining two rings in different directions around the ball.

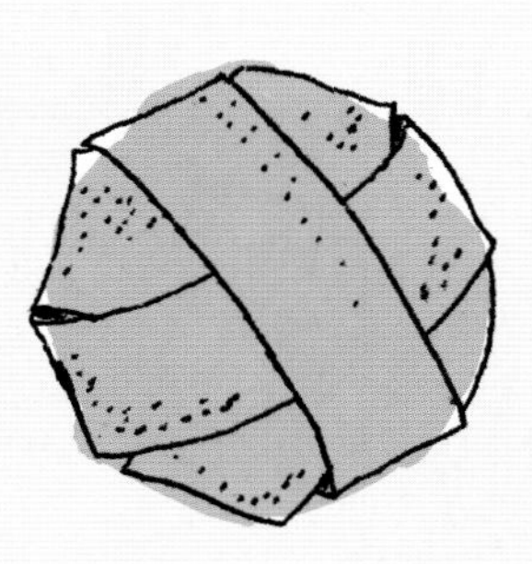

6 Shift the rings around to try to close up all of the holes, and make it more challenging for your hamster to get at the treats inside.

NIBBLE NECKLACE

Here's a great way to give your hamster a chewing workout! Not only is this toy great for chewing but your hamster may also have fun climbing and swinging on it.

HAMSTER TOOTHBRUSH!

This is a great opportunity to provide a variety of textures to help your hamster keep his/her teeth clean, trim and healthy. Including a treat or two can pique your hamster's interest, and the wood and cardboard pieces help to keep hammie's teeth trimmed to the proper length.

TOOLS & MATERIALS

* Hammer and nail, or a drill and drill bit
* Scissors
* String, about 12 in. (30 cm) long

You can use a mixture of any of the following materials:

* Cardboard or corrugated cardboard (no ink)
* Pieces of egg carton
* Slices of toilet paper or paper towel tubes
* Pieces of Popsicle sticks
* Unpainted wooden beads
* Treats

1 Collect a variety of materials, and cut large materials such as cardboard into small shapes. Making a few different shapes will give a nice assortment of edges for your hamster to nibble on.

2 Using either a drill or a hammer and a nail, make a hole near the middle of each one of your pieces.

3 Thread one piece onto the string, slide it to the end and tie a knot around it so that it won't slide off. Then thread the rest of the pieces on, mixing sizes and shapes for variety, and tying knots between pieces as you go.

4 When you have an enticing string of shapes, tie the nibble necklace to one of the bars of your hamster's cage, so that it hangs low enough to reach.

RESTING TOYS

Hamsters love to relax in small and sheltered spaces, which replicate the underground burrows of their natural environment. In this section, you'll discover lots of imaginative hideouts that you can build to keep your hamster feeling safe and secure.

THE HIDEAWAY CAVE

Simple to make, this cave is not only a nice, soft place to take a nap, but is also fun to shred when naptime is over.

A SPLASH OF COLOR
To add a bit of color, you can add a tiny bit of nontoxic paint to the water as you apply the last layer of toilet paper to the balloon.

TOOLS & MATERIALS

* Round balloon
* Toilet paper
* Paper towels
* Water
* Glass
* Large paintbrush

OPTIONAL:

* Nontoxic paint or dye

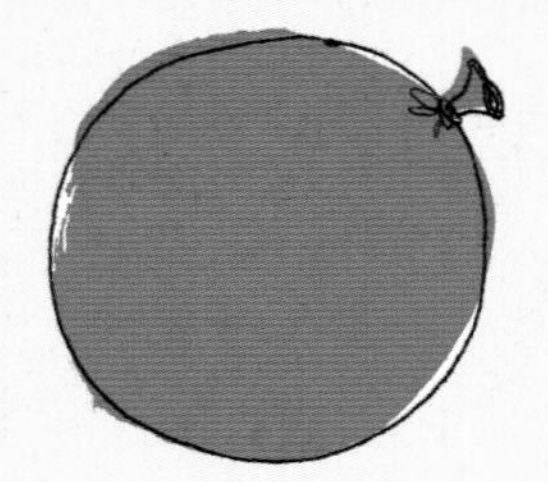

1 Blow up the balloon to the size that you want your cave to be.

2 Use the glass as a stand to hold the balloon. Lay a piece of toilet paper on the balloon, then wet the paper with water, using the paintbrush. Continue adding toilet paper in this way until you have covered the whole balloon, leaving a hole around the knot.

3 Tear the paper towel into strips. Dampen these strips with water and cover the balloon. Continue to add alternating layers of toilet paper and paper towels in this way until you have five layers, ending with a layer of toilet paper.

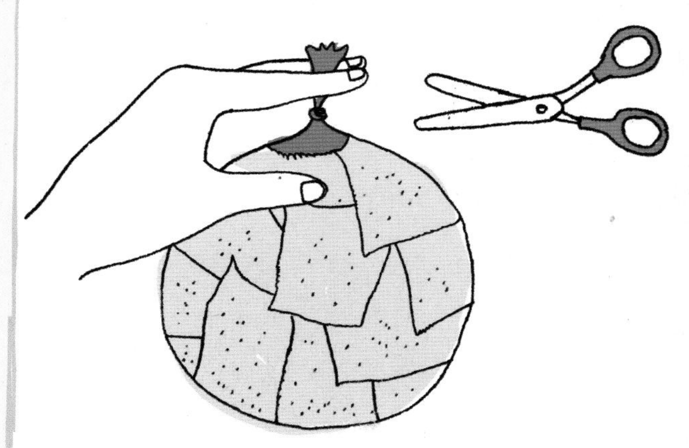

4 Leave the balloon to dry completely. Once dry, carefully cut a small hole in the balloon, near the knot, and let the air out slowly. Remove the balloon from the paper shell.

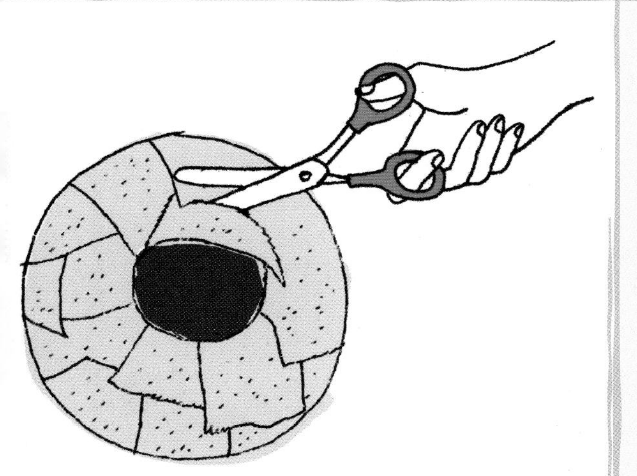

5 Using scissors, enlarge the hole for the door of the cave.

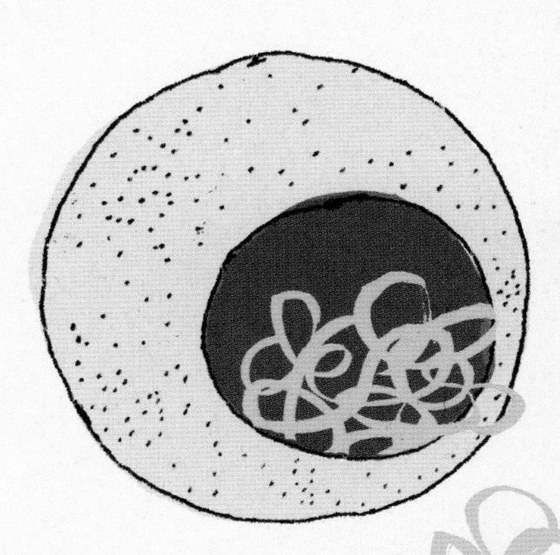

6 Add soft bedding or shredded toilet paper inside the cave.

HAMMIE HILL

This cozy hideout includes a climbable roof for an added challenge for your hamster!

TOOLS & MATERIALS

* Corrugated cardboard
* Jumbo craft sticks
* Popsicle sticks
* Strong, nontoxic glue
* Scissors
* Pencil

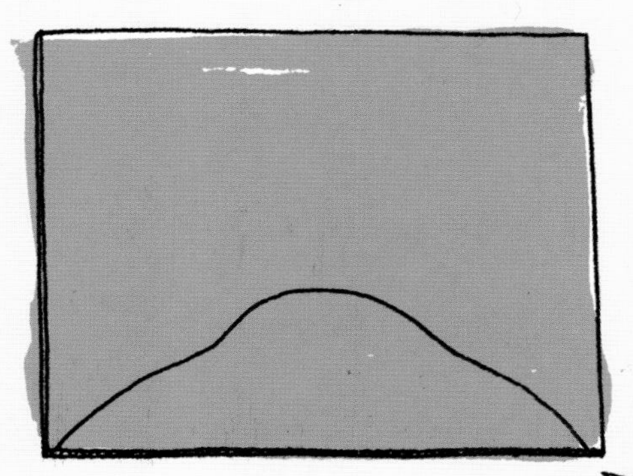

1 On the corrugated cardboard, draw a hill shape that is large enough for your hamster to fit inside comfortably. The bottom of the hill should be the flat edge of the cardboard.

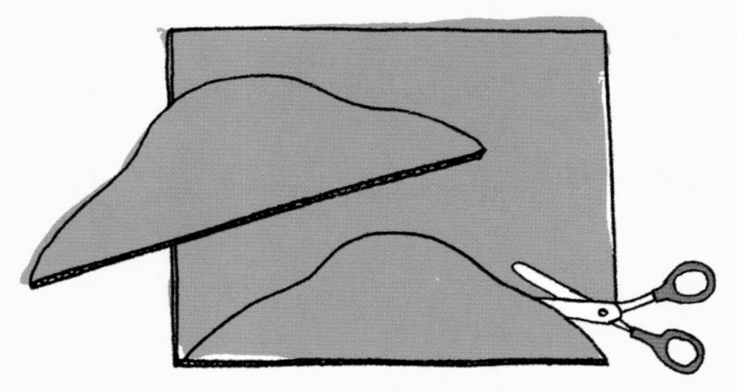

2 Using scissors, cut this shape out, then trace around it for a second hill shape. Cut out this second one. These are the inside walls.

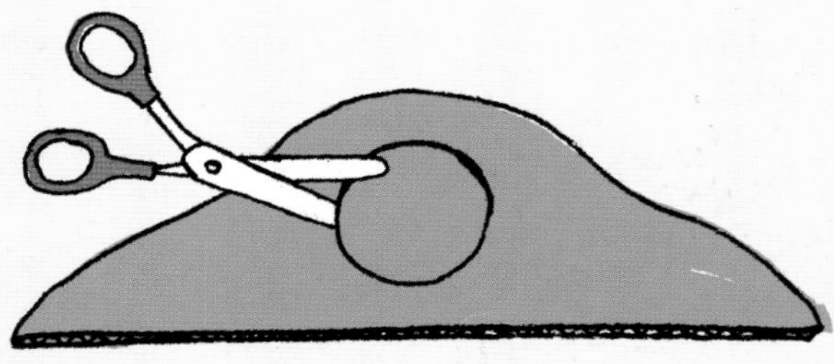

3 Cut out a circle in the middle of one of the walls for a door.

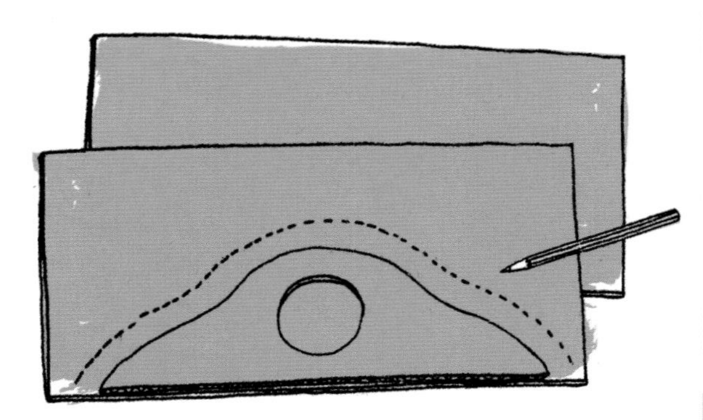

4 To make the outer walls, lay the inside walls on the cardboard, and trace a shape that is an inch or two bigger on the curved side. Trace the door on one of the outer walls as well. Cut out the cardboard outer walls.

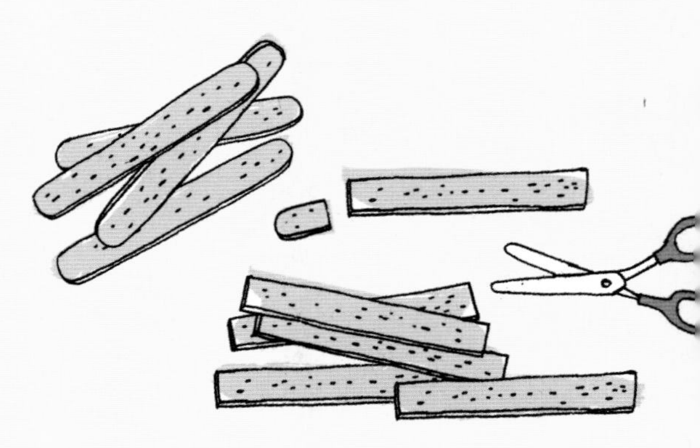

5 Using scissors, trim the rounded ends from enough jumbo craft sticks to cover the top of the hill.

6 Glue these trimmed craft sticks between the inside walls side-by-side, creating the top of the hill.

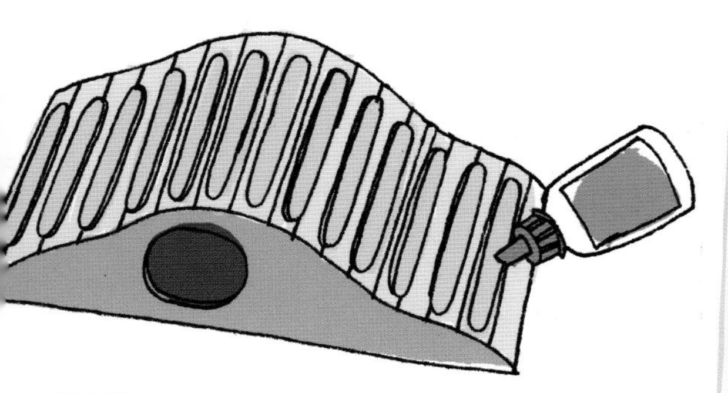

7 Glue Popsicle sticks at even intervals along the top of the hill for treads.

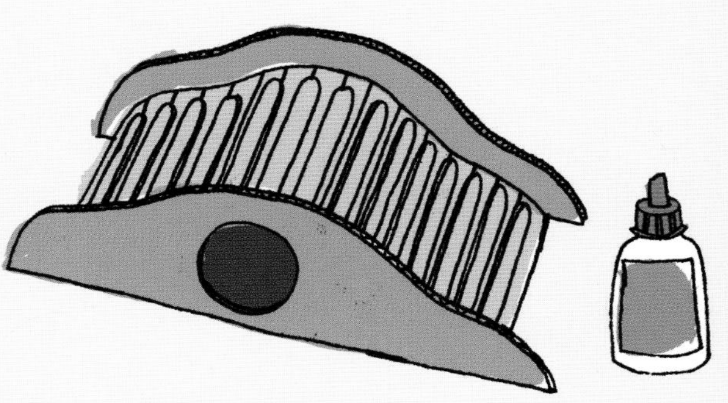

8 Glue on the outer walls, on either side of the hill, matching together the walls with the doors.

TIP

This useful hill hideout can also double as a ladder to reach other levels in your hamster's environment, such as a platform or a suspended hut.

THE CASTLE

Does your hamster deserve a vacation after a long week of running, digging, chewing and napping? This castle is a nice place to get away from it all and relax!

TOOLS & MATERIALS

* Small cardboard box, large enough to fit your hamster (a tissue box works well)
* Cardboard
* 4 toilet paper tubes
* Scissors
* Ruler
* Pencil
* Strong, nontoxic glue

OPTIONAL:

* Nontoxic paints

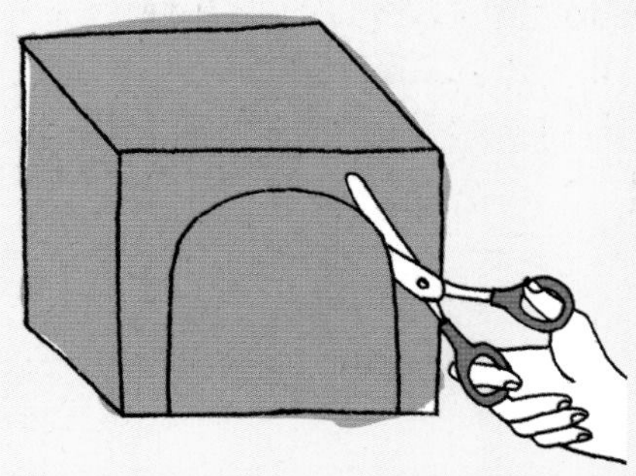

1 Cut a rounded door shape into one side of the small cardboard box or, if using a tissue box, expand the hole to make a door.

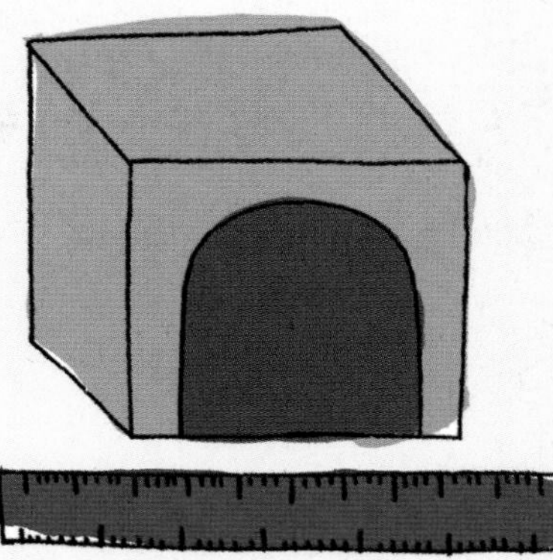

2 Using a ruler, calculate how big you want the four square towers of the castle to be: they should be less than half as wide as the side of the box, and the height should be a couple of inches taller than the box.

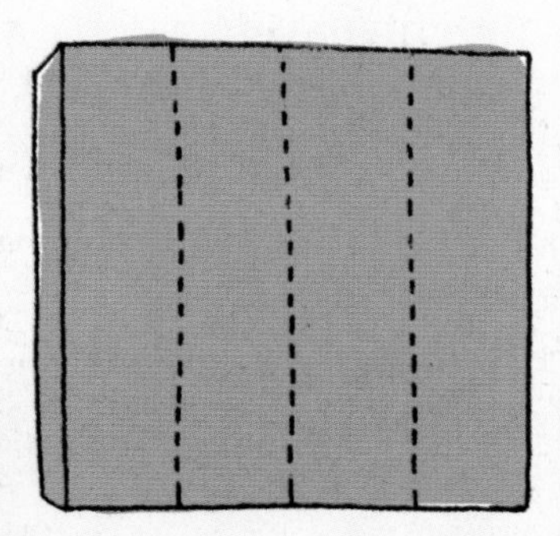

3 Draw a rectangle on cardboard that is the height of the tower and four times the width calculated in Step 2. Divide the width of your rectangle into four equal sections and mark with a pencil. Add on a narrow tab at one end for gluing. Cut out the whole shape from the cardboard. Repeat this three times for the other towers.

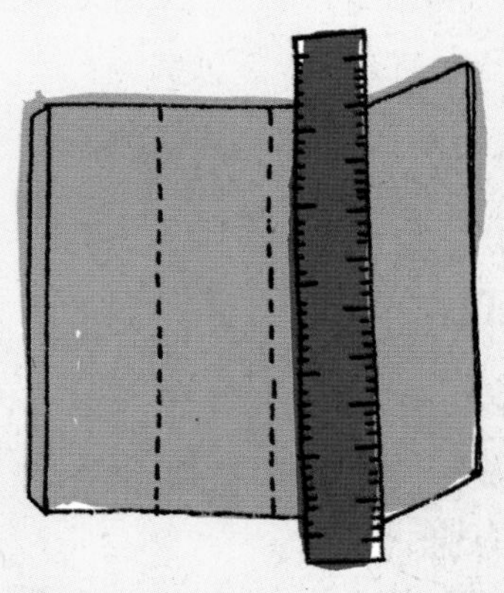

4 Fold the cardboard along the pencil lines. Pressing a ruler on the line and folding up will help you to make a clean fold.

5 Cut rectangular indentations into the cardboard as a design for the top of the towers.

6 Apply glue to each of the tabs and assemble the towers. You can use a piece of tape to hold them together while the glue dries.

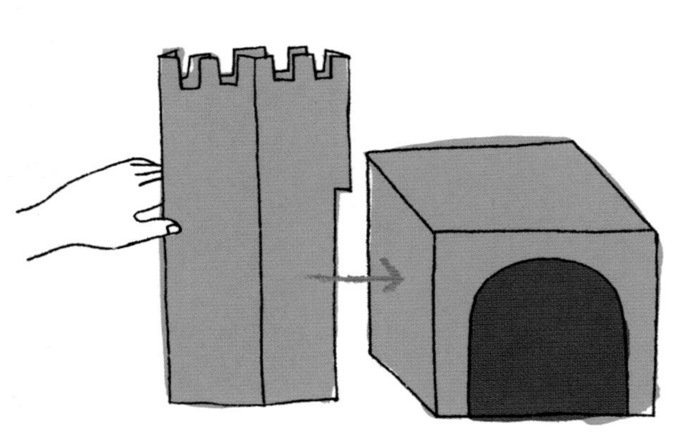

7 Once the glue has completely dried, squash each tower flat, and cut a narrow strip out of one edge from the bottom to the same height as the box.

8 Open each tower up again, slot into place and glue onto the four corners of the box.

9 Make a ramp to the roof of the castle: cut a piece of cardboard to fit between the two towers at the back of the box. Glue narrow strips of cardboard across the ramp at intervals, for treads, and then glue the ramp into place.

10 Cut out three rectangular pieces of cardboard to act as walls on the other three sides of the roof. These should be the width between the towers. Cut rectangular indentations into the top of each piece for decoration. Glue these in place on the three sides of the roof.

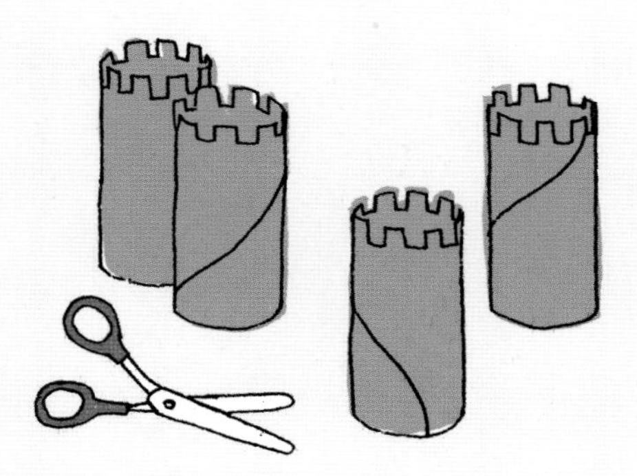

11 Create towers for the outside wall, using the four toilet paper tubes. Cut rectangular indentations into the top of each tube to make a tower design.

12 Arrange these towers around the castle to decide where you want the corners of the outside wall to sit.

13 Measure the distance between these outer towers to calculate how long the wall sections need to be, adding half an inch on either end for inserting into the towers. The walls need to be at least an inch shorter than the height of the towers. Mark this shape on the cardboard and cut it out. Repeat this until you have four outer walls.

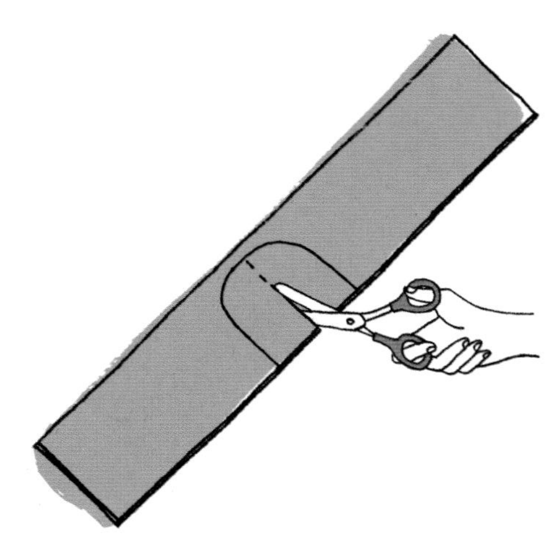

14 On the front wall, draw a rectangle with an arch at the top for the door — this needs to be large enough for your hamster to fit through easily. Draw a line through the center of the door. Cut along this center line and around the arch, and then fold the doors outward.

15 Cut two slots into each of the towers to the same height as the outer walls. The second slot should be one-quarter of the way around the tube from the first. Insert the outer walls into these slots to form the ramparts of your castle.

16 Decorate the castle using hamster-safe paints.

CASTLE COMPLEX
Expand this castle into a complex — add more boxes and expand the wall, or connect multiple castles with tunnels!

THE ROUND HOUSE

Here's a cozy little house with an interesting round shape that makes it extra comfy for a bit of hamster napping.

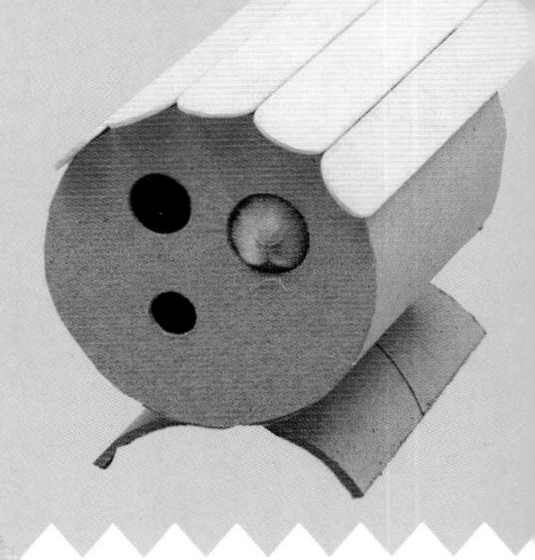

TOOLS & MATERIALS

* Large cardboard tube, wide enough for your hamster to relax in
* Cardboard
* Jumbo craft sticks
* Craft saw
* Scissors or craft knife
* Strong, nontoxic glue

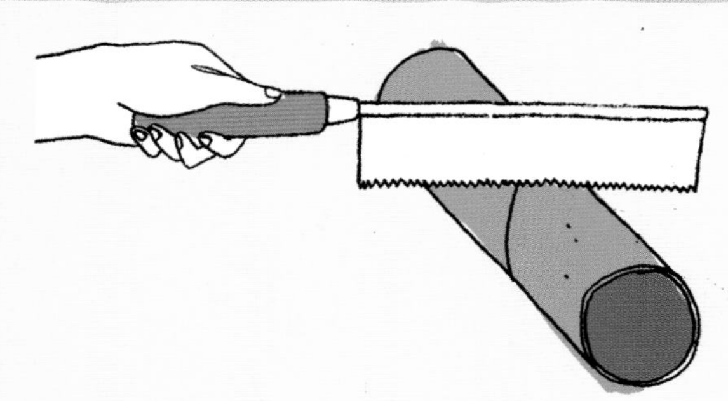

1 Saw off a piece of the cardboard tube to the size that you want the finished house to be.

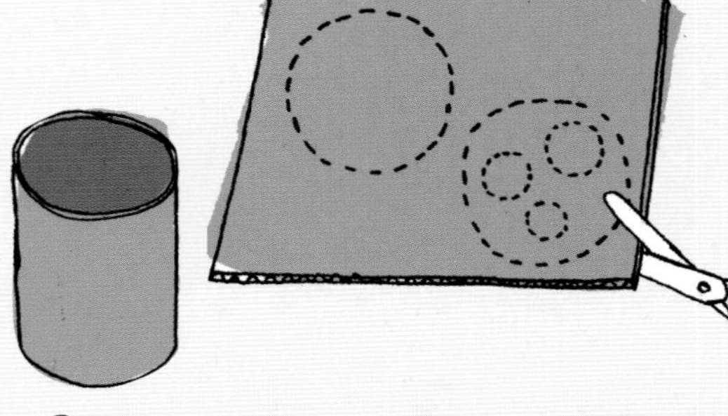

2 On the cardboard, trace around the end of the tube twice to make two circles. Cut out both circles from the cardboard.

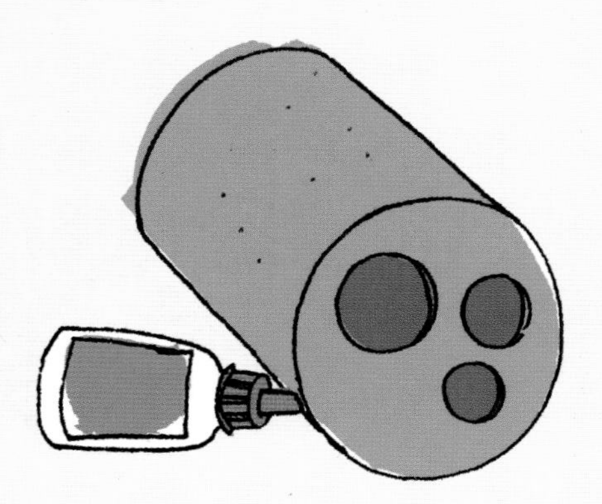

3 In one of the circles, cut out two or three small holes for windows, and glue this onto one end of the cardboard tube.

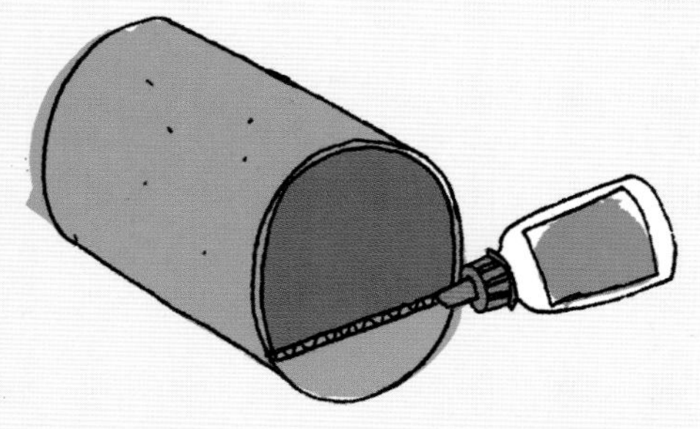

4 From the remaining cardboard circle, cut a narrow slice, and glue this onto the other end of the tube. Make sure that there is still plenty of room for your hamster to get in and out of the tube.

5 Saw off another piece of the cardboard tube the same length as the house. From this piece, cut out a lengthwise section, and glue onto the bottom of the house to act as legs, leaving a small section sticking out to act as a step.

6 Glue some jumbo craft sticks to the top of the tube to make a roof. Welcome your hamster to his/her new home!

THE PERSONAL TOUCH

Personalize the house by adding your hamster's name to the front lip in the doorway.

INDEX

CREDITS

Images courtesy of shutterstock.com
and the following photographers:
Subbotina Anna, page 1;
Hintau Aliaksei, page 3;
Viachaslau Kraskouski, page 13.

Special thanks to our models Casper, Darcey and Syrup.

Casper
Darcey
Syrup